The Golden Chalice

The Golden Chalice

*A collection of writings
by the famous
Soviet Parapsychologist
and Healer*

BARBARA IVANOVA

Edited by Maria Mir and Larissa Vilenskaya

ISBN 0-930420-02-0

Dedication

■ To those courageous individuals in both countries who made this work possible, with special thanks to Henry, Rose, Henry and Zoe.

Contents

Acknowledgements

■ The editors deeply appreciate Mr. and Mrs. Henry Rolfs, Mr. and Mrs. Paul Temple and the Institute of Noetic Sciences for their generous assistance in the preparation of this book. The assistance of Vera Bat-Zvi (Jerusalem, Israel) in translating and editing some of Barbara Ivanova's papers is also highly appreciated. Special thanks to our diligent typesetters, Diana Davis, Jana Janus, and Peyton Curlee, our proofreader Ginger Ashworth, and to Norma Novy for the cover design.

We are grateful to everyone who cannot be named here, particularly those who helped Barbara and others in the Soviet Union to become more acquainted with the world's psychological, parapsychological and spiritual thought by traveling to the USSR. We thank those who brought books and discussed these issues, as well as those who helped us to receive Barbara's writings by substituting for the international mail.

We want to convey our gratitude to everyone who has helped Barbara and us to understand, to grow, and to contribute to improving the quality of life in our world.

The Editors

Introduction

Introduction—
Defining Psi

Larissa Vilenskaya

■ *Psi* research, or *parapsychology* is the field which studies "para-normal" phenomena, e.g. phenomena "which in one or more respects exceeds the limits of what is deemed physically possible on current scientific assumptions." This is an accepted "official Western definition."[1] In the USSR, *parapsychology* is defined as the "field of research studying forms of sensitivity which are not explained by the activity of known sense organs, as well as forms of influence of living beings upon surrounding phenomena, occur-ring without the intermediary of muscular forces."[2] Perceptual phenomena are known as extrasensory perception, which includes such controversial forms of receiving information as telepathy, clairvoyance, and precognition. The unexplored ways of influence that humans, according to psi researchers, can impact the environ-ment are usually termed psychokinesis.

While the exact meaning of the terminology used in this book is explained in the **Glossary**, we would like to emphasize that we view psi research in a broader perspective than these quite narrow definitions. For us, this field deals first and foremost with human potential, with our inexhaustible human possibilities, and with the complicated interconnections within living systems and between living systems. For us, this is also a field which deals with such broad concepts as spirituality, and ascertaining the place and role of humankind in the Universe.

There have been hundreds of books on the subject in general, and many from this latter realm in particular. Our book, however, is unusual since its authors are separated by thousands of miles. (Perhaps this is an appropriate way to write a book about the science of transcending time and space!) This book has three authors or, more exactly, one author and two editors. Our major author, about whom the readers will learn more while reading this book, is Barbara Ivanova, a researcher, teacher, and healer living in

Moscow. Our first editor the readers will know under her pseudonym, Maria Mir. A young psychologist, Maria has traveled once to the Soviet Union and would like to have the opportunity to visit the USSR again; therefore, she prefers to be known by her penname. While in Moscow, she had the opportunity to get to know this wonderful woman, Barbara. Our second editor, Larissa Vilenskaya, is a researcher in psi phenomena who emigrated from the USSR in 1979 and has been a close friend and colleague of Barbara for more than fifteen years. Since 1981, she has been living in San Francisco and is the editor of *Psi Research* journal.

Our book is not a scholarly work, but rather a book of writings. The major issue of the book is not Barbara's theoretical or experimental work in psi research, but Barbara herself—her spirituality, her love for all living creatures, her commitment to actions which will make our world a better place to live in. If, after reading the book, you feel that you would like to talk with Barbara, to share your thoughts and ideas with her, or to ask her advice, then we have achieved our goal. It is often difficult to communicate with someone in the Soviet Union: letters may not arrive; phone calls are expensive, time-consuming and frequently interrupted. Yet, if you feel like writing Barbara, we would encourage you to do so. Your letters and your interest in her work are her protection, her source of confidence, and her reservoir of inspiration and courage which enables her to continue her activities. Her address is: Barbara Ivanova, Prospect Vernadskogo 50-A, Apt. 89, Moscow 117454, USSR; telephone 133-5513.

References

1. Thalbourne, M.A. *A Glossary of Terms Used in Parapsychology.* London: Heinemann, 1982.
2. "Parapsychology," *Filosofskiy slovar'* (Philosophical Dictionary), Moscow: Sovetskaya entsiklopediya, 1980 (in Russian).

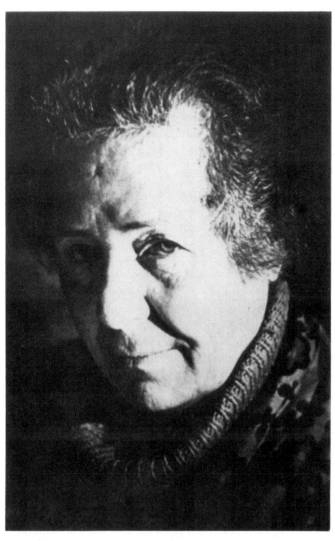

Barbara Ivanova

■ I.

The Beginning

When I used to read fairy tales, I fancied that kind of thing never happened, and now here I am in the middle of one!

Lewis Carroll, *Alice in Wonderland*

Making Friends

Maria Mir

■ San Francisco. New York. London. Moscow. With such an itinerary, Jai and I arrived at SFO with ample time to spare. We unloaded our luggage from the Airporter bus and presented it to the sky cap for checking to Moscow. Looking at Jai's ticket, he said, "You missed your flight—you're scheduled on the 9:00 a.m.—it left forty-five minutes ago!" Arrrrghh.... He then took my ticket, saying, "You're okay. You're scheduled for New York at 10:30; *you've* got plenty of time."

I faintly remembered dashing out of the office as Trusty Tom the Travel Agent called, "Check your tickets, Maria. There have been so many changes, it would be a miracle if they're correct." I had looked quickly at my ticket, and saw that all was in order. I didn't look at *both* tickets....

We catapulted ourselves into the airport, where the ticket agent told us that the earlier flight *had not left* yet due to poor weather in New York, and the 10:30 flight would *also* be delayed. Elementary calculations told us that if the later flight was delayed, we would miss our New York connections, and more importantly, we would miss joining our group in London, miss the flight to Moscow, and only God knew what would happen then. Panic-stricken, we ran to the gate, flashed our tickets at the attendant, rushed aboard the much delayed 9:00 flight and were off! In New York, we walked gracefully from one TWA gate to the next, and again the doors magically closed as we departed—late—for London, hoping that our flight to Moscow would also be delayed. It was.

After a non-stop day of flying from San Francisco, in London we squeaked aboard the British Airways jet under the disapproving eye of the flight attendant to find the nineteen smiling faces of our group, grinning and much relieved by our presence. We were reunited again, and bound for Red Square! We had made all of our connections—people and planes!

3

A long awaited sigh of relief passed my lips as I snuggled into Jai's robust yet receiving shoulder.

"I guess we've gotten the message as to the logistics and timing of the trip!" Jai commented. "Now we know what to expect."

"Yep," I nodded, "it will *look* as though we are right at the edge —over the edge—and things won't work, but, in the end, it will all be perfect! I can relax and know things will work out all right."

"You'll be a lot happier if you do," he said. "And we'll have more *fun!*"

Twenty-one American tourists were now en route to Moscow and points beyond—Leningrad, Tbilisi, and whatever adventures they held for us. Our mission: to make friends with the Soviets; not only with officials and government representatives, but also with common people—citizen-to-citizen diplomacy.

As co-organizer of the trip, I was concerned about managing this large number of travelers with varied interests and strong individual characters, particularly those few who had in one way or another caused an upset in planning for the trip. Would their omnipresent, selfish "me-ism" subside as we entered the Kremlin gates? Would they be able to *feel* the people of the Soviet Union, to go outside of themselves long enough to be able to actually *communicate* with a Soviet citizen? To empathize and listen?

Given the format of the trip, and the focus which had brought the group together (not to mention the harried airplane connections), I could only trust that all would indeed "work out all right." Experience has taught me that when I do relax, things usually work out *better* than my plans. Feeling woozy from lack of sleep and the drone of jet engines, I relaxed into Jai's shoulder and reflected on this assortment of citizen diplomats, bound for the USSR to "make friends."

Eight of us had initially decided to journey to the Soviet Union when we learned that we could travel there for two weeks at the cost of $1,700, *everything* (except vodka and gifts) included. Four months earlier these same eight women had come together to experiment in international telepathy. Our "telEMpathy game" had been quite successful. In the experiment, sitting thousands of miles away from our European counterparts, we had accurately transmitted simple flash card images between our groups. As their group viewed and "sent" us the picture of a red rose, we "received" a red rose. They sent us butterflies, and we received butterflies. We sent them the image of a sun setting behind a mountain, and they

4

accurately perceived our image. They sent us an image of the sphinx and we received pyramids. Later, as we exchanged pictures and results, they gloomily remarked, "We tried to send you the sphinx, but all we could think of was *pyramids*!" Bingo... that's what we had received!

With such success, we were all now unquestioning believers in the powers of the mind, and the efficacy of subtle communication. We were believers in the might of the individual who truly desires peace in the world, and knew that with strong intention and focus, powered by our love for each other and the planet, we could make a difference in the world.

The telEMpathy game had been conceived in the course of a conversation between myself and a dearly beloved friend, Mary. Mary and I had met seven years before during a week long seminar in Northern California. At our first meeting, it felt as though we had known each other for years, as if she were *me* in another body. We spent the week playing like naughty little girls, loving every minute of it — sneaking out of the meetings to sit at the beach and talk for hours, skipping assigned meals to take ourselves to dinner, laughing and giggling and generally sparking the seminar into a joyful state. Before the end of the week, noticing our mutual happiness, our similar size and hair color, people were asking us if we were sisters, noting the only difference between us was the contrast between her crystalline clear blue eyes and my "doe-eyed" hazel. We were truly friends, playmates, confidants.

Years later, we were musing over our long friendship and what had evolved into a telepathic communication — thinking of each other and the phone ringing; thinking of a question I wanted to ask her, and she answering before words were spoken; completing a favor for the other *before* we were asked, and so on. "Do you think it's just because we've known each other for seven years?"

"No, I think it's because we love each other so much. Love must be the medium or carrier of the information, don't you think?"

Yes, we both agreed. Love. Our hearts had the deepest answer, the purest knowing.

"Gee!" we thought, "if it works for *us*, it will work with *anyone* we love, won't it?" Naturally. If the theory was true, it would work with our loved ones anywhere in the world, since neither of us believed that time nor space was a factor in love. As an action-oriented being, I immediately wondered *how* we could try it out — how could we test this splendid hypothesis?

5

Mary was leaving on a European vacation soon, where she would visit friends whom she had known for several years. Specifically, we had a group of friends who were interested in studying healing, and met together three times each week with a teacher to learn techniques for healing themselves and, later, others. Would they be interested in experimenting with us?

A telephone call during their meeting hour affirmed their readiness to experiment in transmitting love. In the course of our conversation, Mary and I had decided that if we were to create such an experiment, we would do it "right." We intended to design a scientifically valid and viable research experiment, which, we grandly concurred, would *demonstrate* the existence of telepathy based on love.

We consulted the foremost researchers in consciousness in the San Francisco Bay Area, including Russell Targ, an expert in remote viewing, and Drs. Jeffrey Mishlove and Carol Irwin at John F. Kennedy University. Jean Millay, Larissa Vilenskaya, and others were also called upon for advice. Painstakingly, we learned about needing "dummy targets" (or pictures) for the judging procedures, and about the tangle of statistics necessary for scientific evidence. We also learned that some of the most successful "telepathy" had occured with "emotionally evocative" targets: dead babies, war-torn amputees, and the like—images that were so emotionally repulsive that (the theory went) the viewer thought, "Guggg, yuck...," the stomach heaved, and a wave of strong feeling sent the information to the receiver. Such a selection of target pictures was wholly unappealing to us, although the theory somewhat corroborated our idea that the emotions are the carrier of intuitive information.

Listening to the avalanche of advice we received, and reading everything we could find, we took what we wanted and left the rest for other researchers. We *did* want it to be scientifically judged, so we created a large "target pool" of pictures, out of which one would be "randomly generated." Concurrently, we had the targets selected by individuals who would not participate in the actual group so that the images would not be "contaminated." (The idea here is that if someone in the sending-receiving group knew all the target images beforehand, they might think of, and therefore send, one of the targets other than the one which had been "randomly generated.") Yet Mary and I definitely did *not* want to send emotionally negative and repulsive targets. Our target-selecting committee was instructed to choose "emotionally uplifting and peace-inspiring" images for our international experiment. Why transmit ugliness? There's plenty already. Positive emotion would work!

After we had fully considered and designed the experiment, Mary took extensive instructions to our European colleagues, and we scheduled the experiment to begin in January, 1983. With them, she determined that we would meet for four weeks, twice each week, and alternate telepathically sending and receiving images. Our experiments would be based both on science and our mutual love of the earth and its peoples.

Together we designed and executed the following format: we met at simultaneous times, 8:00 a.m. for us, 5:00 p.m. for them. Each group came together one half hour before the actual synchronized time, and used the half hour for group sharing and clearing our thoughts. (Gossip and catching-up might be more accurate.) Then, sitting in a circle at precisely 8:30 (or 5:30) we began the experiment by spending five minutes writing in our journals to clear our minds of scatter and extraneous thoughts; five minutes relaxing, with the focus on relaxing the face; five minutes chanting a rhythmic *aum*; and five minutes viewing the team snapshots we exchanged with the other group, tuning in to each individual as well as their collective group energy, as we believed it was. Each five minute segment was punctuated by the ringing of a Tibetan bell. In the course of the weeks, the *aum* became particularly powerful and exhilarating for the group as we felt that our two groups, through intoning the sound, were coming together to become one all-knowing being.

Following this preparation, on the days that we sent a target image, one of us opened the sealed envelope which contained the random target, and set it up in the middle of the circle. We quietly viewed the picture, and then passed it around for each individual to hold and view closely. Each of us then in our own way sent the picture.

On the days we "received" the image, we simply sat in repose for ten minutes, jotting notes, drawing pictures, or simply remembering the images that entered our consciousness. That ended our formal "connection" with our friends. Each team member then completed the notes and pictures they had drawn, filling in colors, feelings, physical sensations and all other phenomena. We spent another half hour sharing our impressions, and compiling a group consensus of the transmission.

Due to our reluctance to send our results through international mail, it was months before we received the hand-carried transcripts from our friends. In that time, it became clear that the actual results were not paramount to the American team. Rather, it was our coming together as a group of relative strangers who had forged a strong bond of friendship and love. Regardless of the results, we felt that we had in subtle ways contributed to international communication, understanding, and peace. It was with this feeling of connectedness and love that we seized the opportunity to travel relatively inexpensively to the Soviet Union. The results of our experiment, which arrived two weeks prior to our planned trip, seemed to confirm our beliefs (although a statistical analysis is yet to be done).

In the course of the next months, twelve friends joined our tour. A film maker, an artist, a businessman, housewives, and Jai, my gentleman-friend, diversified our team and helped us to value the differences between us.

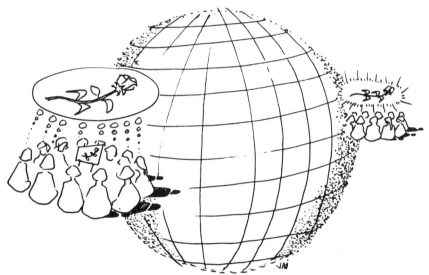

■ Now, here we were, together on a flight to Moscow. Snoozing on Jai's shoulder it still seemed like a dream—Americans coming together for a peacemaking trip to the USSR. There were no agendas, no expectations, only a few names of Soviets given to us by friends. Through the haze of my sleepy mind, the pilot announced that we would land in Moscow in forty minutes.

I roused myself and began to sort out papers and belongings. From a small folder I removed a list of the names of Soviet contacts given me by Larissa Vilenskaya, an emigré from the USSR living in San Francisco. Larissa is the editor of a journal called *Psi Research*, in which she has translated writings concerning psychotronics and parapsychology from Eastern Europe and the Soviet Union. Larissa, formerly a Soviet research parapsychologist, had also assisted us in the telEMpathy game, and, in addition, learned that she and I shared a common interest—healing. With Larissa's help, I was now carrying a list of a dozen Soviet healers, including addresses and telephone numbers.

As I unfolded the list, Jai and I looked over the tangle of names of individuals we might soon visit, playing pronunciation games and laughing at the pretzel-like sounds evoked by the names. Lynn, our tour guide and a dear friend, was soon drawn to our seats by the giggling. "What's going on with you guys—tired from no sleep?"

"No, we're learning Russian—listen, Duuhzzzaa hha oo na Daaa ve taa ssshh vee li!" (Djuna Davitashvili, the reknowned Soviet healer who is reputed to have prolonged Brezhnev's life.)

"Djuna? What *is* that list you have?"

"A list Larissa Vilenskaya gave me of the healers I should visit in the Soviet Union. You know how interested I am in healing, and the Soviets are supposed to be leaders in the field. They're doing lots of research and studies of the healing phenomena."

"Yes, but you can't take that *list* into Moscow!!! If they find it on you in customs, you could get all those people into trouble! The government doesn't like Soviets to fraternize with Americans, and they won't know that you haven't had some sort of secret communication with those people. You could set *back* healing rather than advance it!!"

But what would I do without the list? How could I visit and learn about healing in the USSR? How could I *meet* people there? Phooey. Jai and I quickly set to memorizing the starred names on the list—the personal friends of Larissa who she felt would be particularly open to seeing me, given the risk of meeting with an American.

Looking out of the window, we could see the miles of forests and plains begin to sprout villages, and then cities with huge apartment complexes as we approached our landing in Moscow. Remorseful, and sickened by the paranoia that leads to such lack of communication and warfare, we began to shred the list of names. Quarters, sixteenths, hundredths—we soon held miniscule pieces of papers in our laps. We decided it best to flush them down the toilet, so I wrapped them in a Kleenex and put them into my purse. Rising from my seat, I turned my head, and noticed for the first time that five tall Russian men in dark suits were standing behind me, and had watched the entire shredding process. My American media-inspired paranoia leapt to the fore. Surely, I thought, these were KGB agents. Had they read the names? Had I already endangered the healers? Would I be arrested? Taken to the Gulag never to be seen again? A psychiatric hospital? A chain gang? I grinned sickly and motioned that I wanted to go to the bathroom.

■ With a gulp and beads of sweat on my forehead, I squeezed past the "KGB agents" in the narrow aisle with my treasured shreds. I quickly locked the bathroom door, wishing it were solid steel rather than flimsy plastic. I anticipated the storming of the bathroom door as I frantically began to flush. My heart sank as I watched the pieces of paper stick to the sides of the toilet bowl and gaily float on the returning water. I flushed again and again until the waterlogged shreds of typing paper finally disappeared.

Mission accomplished. I prayed that Jai hadn't already been arrested, and emerged from the bathroom. Looking up the aisle, I saw him in an animated conversation with the five "agents." "Dear, God, they haven't handcuffed him yet!" I thought as I scampered up the aisle to my seat. I found the six men engaged in an exaggerated hand-language conversation tempered by bits of English. The five Russians, members of a trade mission, had been wholly amused and confused by our paper-shredding antics, and were laughing with Jai about our paranoia. As we touched down, we had made friends who proceeded to guide us through the customs rigmarole at the Moscow airport.

Two hours later, our twenty-one member family exited the customs check, bleary from flying and standing, and short several books and papers which were taken by the customs agents. Our intourist guide, Tanya, was awaiting us, dressed in a long black leather coat with a black woolen cap, and vaguely attempting to look cheery on the rainy grey Moscow evening. She escorted us onto the red and white tourist bus and pointed out various sights in the city. We drove past sprawling apartment complexes to the hotel Kosmos on the outskirts of Moscow. Tanya checked us into the hotel, and mentioned that dinner would be over at 9:00. This allowed us fifteen minutes to take our luggage to our rooms, freshen up, and be back down at the dining room.

The Kosmos Hotel, constructed for the Moscow Olympics, is an immense structure built some twenty stories high in a semicircle. The spacious lobby displays elegant metal structures above a white marble floor and mirrored walls. We rode sixteen flights to our room, where to my surprise a quick perusal revealed that we had all the accoutrements: towels, soap, and comfortable—if *very* firm —beds. Toilet paper was available, but its consistency was some-where between tin foil and newspaper, so I was glad to have brought numerous mini-packages of Kleenex.

Remembering our time constraints, Jai and I hurried out of our room and back to the elevator. As we pushed the arrow pointing down, a Russian woman who was stereotypically robust and abun-dant tapped Jai on the shoulder and spoke in Russian, holding her hand out, as if for an offering. "What's she want?" Jai asked me.

"Geez, I don't know . . . a payoff? Why? What did we do?" Then she held up a room key, (which, ironically, is numbered by a cumbersome metal ball affixed to a chain) and motioned that she wanted our key. We quickly learned that this was the "floor lady" —the keeper of the keys. In a Soviet hotel, guests do not keep their keys, but return them to a woman (always) who sits (usually) near the elevator. We wondered what she did with the keys while we were gone.

In the lobby, we trailed our weary group into the buffet dining area, where several friends were already serving themselves rice, a ragged form of beef stroganoff, potatoes, cucumbers, beets, and cabbage. Now, sometime after 9:00 p.m.—it was after 8:00 a.m. by our body's clock, and we hadn't slept for two nights. Yet, the food and the exuberance of our team soon brought the sparkle of adventure back into our eyes. We're actually here!!! *Moscow.*

"Let's take the metro to Red Square!" someone suggested, and by 10:30, a dozen smiling faces had regrouped in the hotel lobby en route to Moscow's famed central square. One among us spoke Russian, so she led our motley crew, too tired to sleep, onto the metro. A splendid mahogany escalator, chandeliers, and marble columns graced the subterranean station, and the greyhaired *ba-bushkas* (grandmothers) were sweeping the floors to an impeccable

11

polish. It truly *was* the world's finest metro. A silent train soon arrived and we sped toward Red Square.

Climbing the stairs out of the metro station, we were greeted by silent streets, devoid of people, with only an occasional taxi passing in the night. Gazing to the south on the quiet night, we saw the glow in the sky which marked the Kremlin walls and Red Square. In the cool spring air, we linked arms and an anticipatory hush fell over the group as we wound our way slowly toward the Square.

In moments, Red Square spread before us. Directly ahead floodlights illuminated the brightly painted onion domes which graced St. Basil's Cathedral—as awesomely detailed and exquisite as any photograph portrayed. To our left, the arches of the Gum department store cast circular shadows on the stones of the Square. And to the right, the walls of the Kremlin—flooded with light and crowned by ruby red electric stars. In the center of the wall we easily recognized the square black marble structure of Lenin's tomb where his body lay enshrined in glass. Alone in the Square, we broke into groups of twos and threes, and walked respectfully to the middle of the Square, quietly realizing the verity of our where-abouts. Behind enemy lines? It was stunningly beautiful.

Standing in Red Square, breathing in the crisp night air and grandeur of the place, I soon heard a strange clippity-clop of booted feet marching toward the Square. Near the wall beyond Lenin's grave I saw three guards marching toward the tomb. It was moments before midnight, and we were about to see the changing of the guard!

The rich grey Edwardian waistcoats, fitted at the waist and full at the thighs, knee-high boots, and classic black fur cossack hats gave an appearance of courtly elegance to the guards, whose somber expressions never changed, even as they were harassed by young children. In a stylish two-count goosestep, their legs kicked up in perfect unison at right angles to the ground as their white-gloved hands slapped the handles of their rifles and chanted rhythmically in the night air. Slap, stomp, slap, stomp, slap, stomp —in perfectly executed turns of military ballet the guards were changed at precisely the moment when St. Basil's chimed midnight. Slap, stomp, slap, stomp—the retiring guards marched crisply away from the tomb as the two replacements stood sober and motionless at the door to Lenin's shrine.

Exhilarated by this performance affirming our whereabouts, we began twirling and giggling in the middle of the Square, mimicking the exaggerated military goosestep and playing Cossack guards. Minutes after midnight, it was a new day—our *first* day in *Moscow*! Playful and exuberant, forgetting the interminable flight, we gathered into arm-linked lines and began to wander aimlessly in the streets, gazing into windows and attempting to decipher the Cyrillic alphabet.

"*Kofe!* That means coffee! Look!" Terry bubbled, "Here's a coffee shop!" The line playfully goosestepped around to look into the windows of a stand-up café, where coffee, tea, and milk were served in a gloomy setting, barren of frills or personality. (Passing the same café the next day, I found it wholly transformed and alive with the chatter of Moscow workers taking their famed, elongated coffee breaks.) We scampered in the empty streets late into the night, until the wear of travel eventually brought sleep sometime after 3:00 a.m.

Too few hours later the group meandered sleepy-eyed into the same dining room to a buffet of sliced cheese, meats, boiled eggs, soft buns, and the ever-present samovar filled with tea. Tanya, officious and contained, met us in the lobby at precisely 9:00 a.m. to begin our "city tour." I wondered how we might reach her, to befriend her, to let her know that we were here on a peace mission —we were *not* the enemy. (It was not long before I learned that the Soviets do not see the American people as the enemy, but are curious and well-informed about us. Unlike Americans, Soviets differentiate between the "people" and the "government," and do not blame one for the mistakes of the other.)

Boarding the bus, I complimented Tanya on her lovely knitted shawl. She methodically recited the store where she had purchased it, with another shallow attempt at a smile. "Poor angel," I thought, "she's probably seen a million American tourists—the Hawaiian shirt and plaid bermuda short vintage, dressed in winter clothes and complaining about the weather."

She had. Her memorized and routinized tour package had been monotoned untold times with scant diversion—the heroes of the revolution, the monuments to the war dead, the museums for revolutionary art, the legends of Ivan the Terrible, the tonnage of the stars atop the Kremlin walls.

At one juncture I pointed to a lovely baroque building, "Oooo! What's *that*?"

"That is *not* important," she snapped.

Yet, despite impending boredom, shutters snapping and eyes glowing, our mad-cap diplomats began to get a feel for navigating the city, as we would in Leningrad and Tbilisi. This was the savvy which would allow us to galavant the streets later, seeking adventure and friends.

Aboard the bus, Jai and I unsuccessfully struggled to remember the names and numbers of the individuals on the list we had destroyed on the plane. In our foggy state (our bodies repeatedly announced, "It's 3:00 a.m.—why aren't you in bed???"), irrespective of the memory games we had played, our efforts were futile. Perhaps a few would strike us later, in a flash of inspiration and memory.

Returning to the hotel, I strolled past a telephone booth when the hoped-for inspiration struck me—I instantly remembered the first and double-starred name on Larissa's list, Barbara Ivanova, and her number! Thank Heavens! I had remembered the most important name on the list!

Barbara had been Larissa's closest friend and work-partner before Larissa emigrated to Israel and later the United States. I happily remembered that I had carried in numerous books and manuscripts for her, and that she spoke English fluently, in addition to six other languages.

I fumbled in my purse for a two kopeck piece and hurriedly dialed the number before I forgot it! *"Allo! Kto govorit?"* a woman answered.

"Barbara?" I asked meekly.

"Yeeeeaaasssss...."

"This is Maria. I am a friend of Larissa Vilenskaya's in San Francisco...."

"Oh, my God!!" she cried, "dear God, I have waited *so long* for this call! Where are you?? Are you in Moscow? Can I see you???!!"

"Yes! Yes!" I bubbled, "I'm in Moscow. I would *love* to see you!"

"Do you have books?"

"Yes, I have many books and articles for you."

"Oh, my God, I have waited so long, thank you! Thank you!" cried her tear-filled voice. I could hear her sobbing quietly into the phone and felt a lump arise in my throat.

"I am so thankful that you have called me. When can I see you?"

"Anytime. Tomorrow?"

"Yes, yes," she sobbed, "please do come, I am so anxious to see you. I have waited so long.... How is Larissa?? I miss her so."

I told Barbara of Larissa's success with her *Psi Research* journal, her speed on the word processor, and her travels and lectures in Europe. We arranged for our meeting at 11:00 a.m. the next day, at Barbara's home. She provided me with detailed instructions via the metro to the stop nearest her apartment.

"Shall I come alone, or may I bring a friend?"

"It will be all right for you to bring one friend, but not more. It would be safer for all of us."

Within the moments of our brief conversation, I felt as though I had known Barbara for a lifetime. Her warmth, sincerity, and compassion surged through the crackling lines and found their way directly into my heart. My throat-lump had not gone away when we hung up the telephone.

I emerged into the street feeling emotional and deeply touched by this beautiful soul. Somewhat faint, I leaned against the booth as tears began to well into my eyes. Such tragedy we inflict on each other. Here were Larissa and Barbara, two beloved friends who were not allowed to communicate, who could not speak on the telephone, took incredible risks to write each other, and would, in fact, never see each other again. I was an intermediary to transmit their love. Why do our governments play this sickening game? Invasions, downed planes, secret troops to innocent nations, creating the *enemy*. The result? Alienation. Separation. Why?

I shook off the tears, and shouldered the responsibility I bore. I knew not where this mission would take me, but I would certainly serve these two friends who were separated by the artificial boundaries of fear.

As I entered the hotel, Jai noticed my swollen eyes, and asked what had happened. "Did you reach her? Is she all right?" I reassured him and briefly relayed our conversation and my resulting emotional state. I quietly invited him to join me the next day — meeting a *real* Russian, a *real* healer. A compassionate soul. He happily agreed.

Tanya was again in the hotel lobby promptly at 9:00 a.m., gathering our depleting numbers for another endless bus ride to some museum or another. I approached her to say that Jai and I would not accompany the group this morning, but had other plans. "What will you do?" she asked.

"Ooohhh, we just want to explore the city a bit on our own...

we're in love, you know, and want to spend some time alone. Moscow is such a wonderful city for lovers," I said.

"Oh. Well, lunch will be served at 1:00, dinner at 7:00," she announced as she mothered her flock out the door to the waiting bus.

I had told only Lynn of our plans to visit Barbara, and had asked her to transcribe into Cyrillic the English address Barbara had given me on the telephone. With the Russian address and metro instructions in hand, Jai and I left the hotel at 10:00, primed for exploration and adventure in the streets of Moscow.

We found our way to the nearby metro station and rode the baroque escalator to the tracks below. There I stopped an unlikely looking Russian fellow and showed him the paper with the name of the metro stop we wished to find.

"*Idemte, ya vam pokazhu*," he said, motioning us to follow him. What luck! He was going our way! We boarded the train and began a sign-language conversation which revealed little but was lots of fun. He guided us onto another train and in a half hour motioned to us that this was our stop. Amazed at our good fortune at finding someone who lived near Barbara, we all gaily exited the train. Our new friend pointed up the stairs, smiled, and promptly walked across the station to catch a train going back to the city center! He *didn't* live here! He had come thirty minutes out of his way to help us find our destination! This is the *enemy*?

Emerging from the metro station, we were greeted by one of the vast apartment complexes we had seen from the air and on our bus ride into the city. Huge, identical, hospital-like buildings stretched as far as we could see. People walked between them on dirt paths, wrapped in warm coats and immersed in their thoughts. An occasional cheery mother pushing a baby carriage brightened the scene, and offered a sense of hope amid the grey sameness.

Barbara's instructions were to walk straight ahead to the "three tall buildings" when we came out of the metro. As we walked, people seemed vaguely curious, yet hesitant to look at us. I wondered if they were being polite or paranoid.... Our smiles, excitement, and the flush of love between us were clearly unusual on the somber streets of Moscow.

One, two, three buildings on the right. The Alcatrazesque grey block structure loomed before us, mysterious and foreboding. Bundling myself against the morning cold and the chill of excitement, I squeezed Jai's arm as we turned up the walk into the building. The lobby was barren and cold and smelled of ancient urine. The elderly babushka who was napping quietly in a straight-backed chair near the elevator awoke as we neared her. We paused and smiled as we approached, wondering if she was the floor lady, the KGB informer of my stereotyped imagination, or simply waiting for something. She gave us no sign, and since we apparently did not need her approval to enter the elevator, we pushed the Up button.

Chafing under her curiously scrutinizing eye and my own paranoia, it seemed hours before the elevator condescended to pick us up on the first floor to carry us to the ninth where Barbara lived. But, already acquainted with "Moscow paranoia," Jai winked at me as he pushed the eleventh floor button. Up we rode with jerky, convulsant motions that threatened to catapult us at any moment to the depths of the elevator shaft. On the eleventh floor, the elevator bell chimed and the doors hesitatingly opened. We then found the stairs and walked down to the ninth floor, pleased at our deception of the "KGB informer" who would now report that two Americans had visited someone on the eleventh floor. We were learning to play the senseless game....

I grumbled quietly to myself as we tramped down the musty stairwell.... I realized that this was the best we could do to avoid danger to Barbara, or our own dreaded trip to the Gulag, yet I was repulsed at having to "play" this paranoid game of secrets, whose apparent results were further alienation and fear between beings. (There is a motto in the USSR which says, "Never introduce one Soviet friend to another. They can't trust each other because they don't know who are the informers.") Hearing my thoughts, Jai reminded me of the "blend" in aikido, in which power is gained by "blending" into the field of the other, and then gently moving them into your field of influence. Knowing that the universe works in its proverbially strange ways, I consented to "play the game."

Winding our way to Barbara's apartment, our feet joined the countless others who had worn through the whitegrey linoleum on the ninth floor hallway.

■ I knocked softly on the charcoal grey door of apartment 89. *"Kto eto?"*

"It's Maria from San Francisco," I responded.

"Yeeaas, just one moment," the voice spoke. I could hear a bolt being unfastened inside the apartment before the door slowly opened the five inches which the chain allowed. A small face peered out from the shadows. Light from the blue eyes looked carefully at Jai. "Who is this with you?"

"This is my friend, Jai. He also knows Larissa."

"Is there anyone else?"

"No. We are alone." We saw the glimmer of a smile as the door closed, and I heard the chain being loosened from its hold.

As if we were in another country, and had just arrived and simply knocked, the door was flung wide and before seeing her face, I was in Barbara's welcoming embrace. Our warm hug of long-lost cousins-found-again told me that I had known her for aeons. I squeezed her, feeling the strength in her small but supple frame, and tingling from the love and gratitude which flowed from her chest into mine. I knew unquestioningly that I was in the right place at the right time. We hugged for long moments, sharing our wordless and poignant feelings. Then her strong hands grasped me gently by the shoulders and she straightened her arms to look at my by-now-unimportant face.

She veritably glowed. A five foot, two inch power-packed house of energy, her blue eyes sparkled, and she grinned broadly as though it were Christmas and Santa had brought her a spotted pony. "I am so happy you are here...." We held hands as we looked at and remembered each other. "And Jai, I am pleased to meet you," she said, reaching her arms to his shoulders for the welcoming hug. "Please, come in!"

In two short steps we were around the corner into the living room of our first Soviet apartment (also the dining room, bedroom, and dressing room). The tidy order, cleanliness, and warmth of the small room was a dramatic contrast to the outside streets and the lobby of the building. Clearly, I was now *inside* Mother Russia, in the home and heart of her people. The walls were adorned with icons and pictures of Jesus and animals. A cot-like bed was pushed against the wall of the room beside a large table on which was the only clutter in the room—a typewriter, and mountains of papers and books. Book shelves and an ancient overstuffed armchair (which was also a folding bed) completed the furniture. The chair was situated to look onto the narrow balcony, which, to my surprise, was abundant with newly potted plants and flowers, from which the pigeons were now gaily plucking the seeds.

There was little room to move about, so Jai sat himself in the armchair as I set my bundle of books and papers on the table and squeezed as gracefully as possible over to the windows. "Your plants and flowers are beautiful! I haven't seen many houseplants around Moscow."

"No, some people think I'm strange for growing them, but I love them so. I talk to them and they grow very well, even in the cold!" Intuitively she knew what some scientists were only now beginning to investigate in their sterile laboratories—that plants respond in subtle ways to loving kindness and care.

"OOOhhhh!! Are these the books you have brought for me? So many!"

"Yes, some are from Larissa and others are books which I thought you might enjoy about healing throughout the world."

Barbara moved respectfully to the pile of materials I had delivered, as if approaching the high altar at Lourdes. Tears welled in her eyes as she slowly and tenderly looked at the title of each treasured piece. I was Santa, and I had delivered an entire stable of spotted ponies.

I was profoundly grateful now for the brief meditation I had conducted with myself before entering the customs gates. "... I will pass freely. All the books I have will be delivered safely to my friends in the Soviet Union. I will pass freely." I did. (Others of us had been detained for up to one hour and searched in agonizing detail. Several of our group had books, letters and manuscripts taken away.) And now I saw how infinitely precious these books were to Barbara, as if they were original manuscripts of life and hope written by Columbus from the New World.

We sat in silence as she caressed each source of information, weeping softly with gratitude and delight. Jai reached out and took my hand, squeezing it and catching my eye with a twinkle. To be present at a moment like this, having brought love and communication from halfway around the world, was not the burden of responsibility I had anticipated, but a gift of the highest magnitude. Deeply thankful for the opportunity to experience this moment, I winked back at Jai through the joyful tears of my own gratitude. His shy smile told me he felt the same. Time stopped.

Minutes or hours later, Barbara turned to us from what seemed the lifetime stash of Christmas presents we had brought her. (I later learned that because of her fluency with the various languages and her voracious appetite for scholarly information, she read, assimilated, and wrote about the entire set of manuscripts in less than two months!)

19

"It is very kind and brave of you to have brought me these books. You know, it is impossible for me to receive this information about parapsychology that I so long for. I often feel that I am working in a vacuum and have no knowledge of what is happening in science throughout the world. It would be so fine if we could freely share our knowledge for the betterment of human kind. Perhaps one day our governments will not be so threatened and they will allow this. I work toward it in my own small way."

"Yes, I know you do, Barbara. Even in the United States I know of your work." From Larissa, I knew that Barbara, born in 1917, had spent the majority of her years teaching and conducting research into clairvoyance, precognition, and healing. She had taught healing to groups of young practitioners who now operated in the vast underground movement of healers in the USSR. I had read several of her numerous manuscripts carried out by Larissa when she left for Israel two years before. And I had read the sensationalized articles in the *National Enquirer* about the "remarkable Russian telephone healer" who healed patients by talking with them on the telephone.

"I want to learn more about your work, Barbara."

"Yes, yes, of course. But, first, let me get us some tea." She moved with quick and sure steps around the corner.

I sighed and closed my eyes to sense the vibration and energies of her home. Quiet. Peaceful. Lonely. Busy. Protecting. Mysterious. Healing. Healthy. Safe. Secure. I opened my eyes to see a large golden painting of Jesus glowing and gazing lovingly at me. Jai, visually artistic and creative, had already surveyed the painting and was studying in detail each feature of the apartment: the small icons in baroque frames which spoke of generations of Russian tradition; the tattered but neatly tucked green blanket on the bed; a soft pillow with hand-knitted cover; what appeared to be a diploma with a red seal; the photographs and cartoons of cats and kittens which festooned much of the wall; the dictionaries in innumerable languages: Russian—English, Russian—French, Russian—Portuguese.... On the table countless papers inscribed by a faded ribbon revealed immeasurable hours of labor at the typewriter. Taking one of the dog-eared bundles, I began to read the faint type. It was captioned: "Meaningful Messages in Dreams."

"Hey, look. I've got a friend!" Jai said happily. I turned to see him stroking a huge tabby cat, marked with white collar and feet, draped languorously across his lap.

"Ooohhhh, what a beautiful puss!" I exclaimed.

"Oh that's Yashka! Be a little careful of him," Barbara called from the kitchen. "He loves to play, particularly with men for some reason, and he sometimes forgets he has sharp claws!" Naturally, this admonition started Jai immediately egging the cat to play. In the wastebasket he found a crumpled piece of paper and tossed it onto the bed. The cat leapt from his lap and the chase was on! Coming out of the kitchen Barbara nearly tripped over the bigger-than-life feline as he chased the paper ball into the hall. "Oh, he has found a playmate now!" she laughed, balancing the tea tray with acrobatic skill.

We pushed aside papers on the table to make way for the tea tray as the cat continued to bat the paper ball around the floor of the small room. "You certainly are quite a cat-lover, Barbara!" I commented, having noticed the hundreds of cat pictures and this huge, healthy feline who was charging recklessly around the room in pursuit of his paper "mouse."

"Yes, I do love cats, and all animals. Yashka brings me such joy." As if hearing his cue, the cat leapt onto Barbara's lap and climbed nimbly onto her shoulder. "This is his favorite place to sit! Would you guess that he is seventeen years old?"

"No!" Having watched Yashka cavort around the room, bounding onto book shelves and window frames, it was impossible to believe this was anything other than an overgrown kitten. "What is your secret of kitty youth?" I asked Yashka.

"Ohhh, we have no secrets, only love!" Barbara laughed. "I do give him healing energy each day, though, and he seems to know just how to use it!" she said, gently stroking the loved one who was now stretched across her bosom onto her shoulder. "Here, I have written a paper about my work with animals!" she said, fumbling through the manuscripts to find one entitled *Psi in Animals*.

"Yes, I would love to read this. But, now that I am here with you, please tell me about your work. I have read articles about you, but I never knew how accurate they were. Do you work with Jesus?" I said, commenting that I was surrounded by pictures of the man from Nazareth.

"Well...uummmm...we work with the higher forces," she replied, looking into the corners of the room as though the fabled listening devices were tuned into our conversation at this very moment. "He is one of them."

"Is our conversation being *bugged*?" I whispered.

"I don't know... but I do not have to worry about my conversations." She was grinning. "They have tried several times to put me into a madhouse—but the Higher Forces helped me. I hope they'll help me further, in other similar cases which might occur."

"Does that really happen? They just knock on the door and take you?" I said, evincing the naïveté of my war baby generation that had not experienced such horrors.

"They do it in different ways."

I heard her words, yet was unable to fully integrate the reality of the situation. I could not imagine living in fear that somebody would take me in the street, or knock on my front door and simply take me away to a mental hospital. I did not viscerally believe that this behavior was a part of the "Civilized World" in the 1980s.

"But this is not my concern! I know I will be protected!" she smiled.

"Yet, but it's not Jesus who protects you?" I was still confused by the pictures throughout the room.

"Yes, it *is* Jesus, but not *only* Jesus. He has help, if you will. The specific personality by which we know a person on the earth plane is insignificant in the other realms. Many people must cling to a particular person or name to assist in their evolution. I simply feel the energies of the higher, more intelligent forces that guide the universe." Barbara was now pouring tea with queenly grace as she spoke the words of a monk. I was fascinated by this woman— the body of a Russian babushka, the wisdom of a sage, the heart of a mother, the soul of a saint.

Departing temporarily from the esoterics, we spoke of our mutual friends, and I reported to Barbara of the recent news in the field of international parapsychology as I knew it. I now wished I had more thoroughly studied the numerous newsletters and journals I received, since she hungered for knowledge. What were the new theories? What research was underway? Were there recent studies proving the reality of the subtle realms? I was glad to share the results of my own telepathy experiment, which had brought my group to the USSR. She was delighted, and told me details of an experiment she had conducted with Professor Sochevanov (a geologist quite interested in dowsing) in an attempt to use dowsing techniques for indicating the influence of healing energies.

At one point in our Russian tea ceremony, I admired the unusual tea strainer Barbara used. It was a very simple, small aluminum strainer whose short arm slipped into the spout of the tea pot. As the tea was poured, it passed easily through the strainer into the cup. "What a marvelous invention!" I noticed. "I've never seen such a strainer!"

"Oh! You must have one—I have another!" Barbara exclaimed, squeezing her way into the kitchen. She returned in seconds with a new strainer and handed it to me. I had learned the reality of a deeply rooted Russian custom: when one person admires the possessions of another, the article is *given* to the person who admires it. The lesson was later confirmed when I thoughtlessly admired the woolen scarf of a newly-found friend in Tbilisi. Before I could finish the sentence remarking how lovely the scarf was, she had it off her shoulders and around mine. I did not want to take the scarf or the tea strainer from people who obviously had so little, yet neither woman allowed me to refuse her gift. Throughout my stay in the Soviet Union, I was haunted by the mystery of this tradition—in America, the "land of plenty," we know little of giving, and we hoard our possessions as though our lives depend upon owning things. Here, in this cold, barren land where so little is available, the people *give* freely what they possess. Their lives depend not on having, but on giving, and the pleasure derived from it....

I reluctantly accepted Barbara's simple gift. We chatted and sipped tea for an hour, talking of Dr. Krippner and the psycho-tronics conference, remote viewing experiments, *Psi Research* and Larissa, cats and kittens, politics and religion. It felt as though we were moving through the layers of our personalities to reach the point where we could share our deeper beliefs and attitudes, our theories and practices of the healing art.

I shared the knowledge I had gained from living over one year in Brazil, studying with healers and "psychic surgeons." She knew about psychic surgery, but had never seen it practiced, and was fascinated by my phantasmagorical, but true, tales. I told her about the small village in northern Brazil, where I had seen a friend's film of a young woman performing heart surgery on an elderly Indian by cutting open his chest with a pair of kitchen scissors as he lay, fully conscious and free of pain, on her table. Pulling apart his chest cavity and revealing the ribs, she thrust her hand into his torso and quickly removed a pulpy mass of dark tissue. She tossed the bloody tumor into a wastebasket and then placed her hands on the outside of his chest, pressing to close the twelve inch wound. Smiling, the man got up from the table and walked home. When he was filmed several days later, he appeared ten years younger and brazenly opened his shirt to show the hairline scar down the center of his chest.

Her next patient required brain surgery, and, were the same operation not on film, I would scarcely believe it. A young man, his eyes glazed and out of focus, lay on his stomach atop her metal surgical table. She removed the kitchen scissors from her pocket and began to cut away at his skull with some difficulty. The blood streamed from his open wound onto the foot rest at the bottom of the surgical table. Fully conscious, and obviously feeling no pain, the fellow put his finger into the blood and began to play tic-tac-toe!! Another mass of tissue was removed and tossed into the basket, and the man was soon up and smiling. His wife was in tears and muttering, "*Obrigada, obrigada a Dios,*" as he placed his arm around her and left the clinic.

Barbara listened intently to these stories, nodding agreement and approval. "Yes, I have read of such phenomena, but I have only met Prof. Hans Naegeli from Switzerland, Prof. Hans Bender from Germany, and Dr. Stanley Krippner who could tell me first-hand stories. And tell me, how do you explain these seemingly impossible feats?"

Sensing that my answer might determine the depth to which Barbara would reveal to me her own knowledge, I felt as though I had been catapulted onto the cosmic testing ground. I remembered the wise words of a friend, José, who once told me, "Hesitate, Maria. Before you speak, count to ten...." I breathed and cleared my mind by counting slowly to ten.

"I find the answer to these mysteries explained by the new physics," I said. "I think we are all made of atoms vibrating in space, and our shape and form is determined by the particular frequency and composition of our atomic structure. And I believe that our human will power and intention are capable of rearranging and reorganizing atomic structures. I think these healers, who have disciplined in themselves a strong willpower and intent, and are motivated by love of people and of the planet, can enter the atomic frequencies of the patient and restructure the sick tissue into its natural healthy state." It seemed too rudimentary and simplistic an explanation for the multifold phenomena I had observed.

"Yes, you know that it is the power of love that heals," Barbara grinned. "I have found this is true."

"How does it work for you?" I asked cautiously.

"Here, let me show you!" she said, bouncing up from her seat.

■ "You watch while I give Jai a treatment, and I will tell you what I am doing as I work!" Barbara looked as though she had just received another stable full of spotted ponies. Her sparkling eyes reminded me of last night's Russian champagne—she was in her element and doing what she knew best.

She winked at me and went into the kitchen to return with a small, straight-backed chair. We pushed the large armchair out of the central position in the room, and she set the smaller chair in its position facing the balcony.

"I must be able to walk around the subject, and that chair is so big!" she said, motioning to the overstuffed beast which the cat now enjoyed.

"We must have fresh air—I hope you won't be too cold," she said, opening the balcony window an inch or two. "The air keeps circulation in the room and allows us to use the ultra-violet energies. Also the toxins can leave the room this way and return to the ethers."

She then directed Jai to sit in the chair, feet apart, with his hands resting on his knees and palms up. "And keep your spine straight," she admonished, "so the kundalini energy can flow easily." She stood quietly beside him, her hands hanging naturally together in front of her, and bowed her head.

Barbara was silent for a few moments. When I later asked her what she had been doing, she explained, "I am asking the higher forces to assist me. I am asking to be a clear and pure channel for the highest energies. And, most importantly, I am asking that I do not interfere with the karma of this individual, for each person must heal himself according to the greater laws of the universe. I do not wish to interfere. Some individuals are learning their life lessons through the disease process. In these cases, it is not good to interfere."

Barbara then raised her hands over her head with her palms up, and wiggled her fingers as though she were materializing a cup in the air. She told us, "I vibrate my fingers until I begin to feel a prickling sensation at the end of them, which tells me that I am connected to the higher forces. Then, I imagine a *golden chalice* full of light and love." Gazing up to her hands as though they were lifting a grail filled with holy elixir, she said, "This golden chalice is filled with light, and love and energy. It is this energy which will heal Jai, not me."

Then she moved her hands down toward his head and chest, keeping her palms six to eight inches from him at all times, which, she said, gave her hands "freedom to act for themselves." Like a perfect mime, it appeared that she was drawing energy from the chalice down to Jai, and then, with her fingertips, directing it into his body. I noticed Jai shiver.

"I free myself of thoughts, and only channel the energies into his body. *I* do not know how he needs to be healed. I am simply the vehicle for the higher forces to work their magic of healing. It is my job to stay clear of judgements, thoughts, and opinions, or thinking that *I* know what to do!"

Jai, whose artist's eye is incessantly scanning the world, closed his eyes with a sigh, breathed deeply, and straightened his shoulders.

"How are you feeling?" Barbara asked him.

"Ummm... very peaceful and relaxed. And warm."

Barbara continued to move her hands in slow arcs near his body as she moved around the chair. "I am simply allowing the energies to pass through me into him, and directing them through my hands. My hands are now very hot so I know it is working. How are you feeling now?"

"Ummm... like I could fall asleep but there's too much happening."

She began to focus her hands at Jai's neck, moving them to a distance three or four inches away, and swinging gentle circles from front to back. I smiled as I remembered that Jai has a chronically stiff neck, and regularly jerks his neck to relieve the cramping. Barbara caught my smile and looked at me. "So, you think we have found the spot?"

"Well, perhaps," I answered, "see what you think."

"Yes, he does have blockages here in his neck which are preventing him from full awareness of his body-vehicle. It also closes down his heart-chakra and emotional body."

I nodded my head, remembering Jai's earlier comments about not knowing his body and emotions. Jai was nodding, too. "You're right," he told Barbara. "I know nothing about emotions. It's like I have one faint highway into my heart, and it's unavailable most of the time. Women seem to have an entire *roadmap* of emotions. Yes! Open the gates!"

Barbara smiled and again closed her eyes, focusing energy into Jai's neck. Jai shivered throughout his body. "Wow! What a shot of energy!" he exclaimed. "What *are* you doing???"

"How do you feel now?"

"Very full and tingly. Yet peaceful and relaxed. My body feels a little shaky."

Barbara had been working for approximately one or two minutes on Jai.

"It would be good for you to lie down for a few minutes."

As Jai lay on the bed for several minutes, Barbara moved to wash her hands, noting that she wanted to be cleansed for each client. "Do you wash so that you will not be contaminated, or so that you will be fresh for the next client?" I asked, as she moved for the bathroom.

"Oh!, no," she laughed. "I do not have to worry about being contaminated, I am protected by the Higher Forces! I do not take on the illnesses of the patient!" Chuckling, she added, "You know I never much understood the belief systems in which the healer had to take on the patient's disease... seems silly...." Shrugging her shoulders, she closed the bathroom door.

Jai appeared to take a lovely two minute cat nap and arose with a grin on his face. "I feel *great*!! Thanks for the new neck, Barbara! My body *feels* so good! It *feels*. That's a breakthrough!" he laughed. "Okay, your turn!" he said, motioning to me.

I sat in the smaller chair as Barbara emerged from the bathroom and Jai began sketching on his omnipresent drawing pad. Yashka, fully aware of the goings on in the room, was curled up and napping directly underneath the chair. No wonder he looked so healthy!

"Hummm... you are very healthy, I see," Barbara said, as she again paused momentarily and then raised her hands above her head and vibrated her fingers, creating the golden chalice. "Let's see, I will have a different intention for you. We will see if it works!"

With that, she began moving her hands in the same arcs inches away from my body. I began to feel the sense of relaxation, peace, and warmth that Jai had commented upon.

"How are you feeling?"

"Umm... warm, tingly, relaxed, I feel happy."

She continued moving in the arcs for perhaps two minutes.

"How are you feeling now?"

I felt as though I had just taken a bath and then a cold plunge.

My being felt both cleansed and stable—the tautness and strength that one feels after a sauna and cold tub. I told Barbara what I felt.

"That's it!" she smiled, "I wanted to cleanse you and protect you for your journey in my country. To make you feel both open and wondering, yet strong and secure in yourself."

I nodded. A very subtle difference, but it worked. I felt fully energized and awake, and found no need to rest as had Jai.

Jai and I were sharing a sense of euphoria and overall well-being after our healing sessions. The conversation reached a pause, when as if on cue, there was a knock at the door.

"Oh, that must be Nikolai," Barbara said, smiling and squeezing past the chairs to the door. "Nikolai?" she questioned.

"Da! Varvara, eto ya."

I again heard the chain unfasten from its lock. Nikolai, a young Russian in his mid-twenties, of slight build with light brown, baby-fine hair draping into his large, round hazel eyes, soon entered the room.

"Nikolai, poznakomtes, eto Maria, eto Jai." Barbara said, indicating an introduction. "Nikolai doesn't yet speak English, but he is learning!"

Barbara spoke a few words to the young man in Russian, then he graciously excused himself and went into the kitchen.

"Nikolai is going to fix us some lunch! He is a very good cook! Nikolai comes here once a week to help me in our work and study healing. He visits me on weekends and then returns to his work."

"How do you do your telephone healings that have been so well publicized in the West, Barbara?" I asked her.

"I do it the same as I have shown you. When people telephone me, I concentrate on sending them energy."

"Through the telephone lines?"

"No, directly to them. The telephone only helps me tune into where they are. And I can tell a great deal about their illness through their voice. We all have different gifts, and the remote healing works very well for me. I also love to teach. We are all healers and need only to develop and discipline the skill in ourselves."

Barbara began to show us her file of articles from European nations that told of the telephone healings she had successfully accomplished. West Germany, Sweden, Italy....

In what seemed like a few minutes, a smiling Nikolai appeared from the kitchen. *"Obed gotov,"* he said.

"Lunch is ready!" Barbara translated.

She escorted us into the kitchen, again, a spotlessly clean room, four by six feet with a small table at one end. The kitchen was well lit since it faced the balcony, and the table, bountifully decorated with plates and serving bowls, was cheery.

Jai and I squeezed precariously into the double corner seat, allowing Barbara and Nikolai access to the sink and mini-stove, where steaming pots were bubbling. A meal unlike any I have ever had was served with the grace and style of Catherine the Great: boiled potatoes, noodles, and brown bread. "I was very lucky to find some butter in the store last week!" Barbara exclaimed delightedly, dabbing the last few tablespoons carefully onto the noodles. Unmistakably, the cupboards had been cleared of their last treasured morsels, and offered graciously to the guests. Jai and I ate sparingly, sensing for the first time the tragedies of economic hardship that we read about in the American press.

I felt a lump arise in my throat as I thought of the contrast between the abundance of the hotel buffet, laden with delicacies, and the "foreign currency" dining rooms in the hotels that offered sumptuous meals to foreign tourists, paying in the coin of their land. Russian citizens were not allowed into tourist hotels. Nor did most foreign tourists venture to the supermarkets for the Soviet citizens, but went instead to the lavishly stocked *Beriozka* stores, where, again, Soviet citizens were not allowed, and where only foreign currency is accepted.

"The noodles are perfectly cooked, 'al dente'," I smiled to Nikolai, as Barbara translated my compliment.

"Oh! I remember we have a special treat for our guests!!" Barbara exclaimed. *"Podozhdite,"* she said, pointing to the small balcony door. Nikolai rose from the table, and managed to open the door enough to reach his hand outside. His hand reappeared grasping two very dried and stiff fish. "These are *vobla*. They were a gift from a friend whom I healed. They are so delicious! Here, try it!"

She adroitly snapped off the heads, and began peeling the skin and flesh from the bones, placing a piece on each of our plates. Tasting it, I found the smoked fish savory, if slightly salty, and a compliment to the bread.

We chatted lightly through lunch, with Barbara translating our comments to Nikolai, a sweet, gentle soul, whom I would trust to cure any ill I might have. For dessert, Barbara offered us what was surely the last item in Mother Hubbard's cupboard, a two inch block of the mild white cheddar cheese which is popular in the Soviet Union. She had no refrigerator, so again, she went to the balcony to retrieve the cheese. I wondered what happens in the dark of winter....

Barbara refused our offer to wash the dishes, and we returned to the living room. We heard the muffled sounds of Nikolai washing the dishes. He shortly followed us into the room, where, with a nod of his head and a quiet, *"do svidaniya,"* he excused himself.

"He must go now," Barbara said, and followed him to the door.

"What is it we can do for you, Barbara?" I asked. "I want to help you in whatever way I can. Shall we bring you some food from the *Beriozka*?"

"No-o-o," she laughed, "they sell only caviar and luxury foods there. Russians can never eat such foods! It would spoil us! Those were the 'good old days!'" Her good nature astonished me, as she demonstrated a compassion for the foibles of humankind which indeed surpassed my understanding.

"Well, what then?" I was driven to find a way to assist this beautiful soul.

"Oh, I have everything I need. You have already done the thing which is most valuable to me by bringing this information about parapsychology from the West. I have nothing to ask of you."

"Do you even have a *dream* that I can help along? Shall I invite you to a parapsychology conference?"

"No, I would never be allowed to leave the country."

"Please, do think of something... It would mean a great deal to me."

"The only dream I have these days is to have a book of my writings published. And, regrettably, this can only happen in the West. It is very difficult—impossible—to have a book about parapsychology published here. But, I think to have a book published, even in the West, is not an easy task."

"No, it is not. But I would like to try. I think Larissa will help me and together perhaps we can publish a small book of your writings."

"Oh... that *would* be a dream come true...." she sighed.

We spent the next hour before our departure sorting through the papers and manuscripts which are included in this volume. Barbara's excitement mounted as she gave me page after page of her writings, and a bibliography of articles about her and by her that had been published in other countries. I was leaving with as many papers as I had brought!

I asked Barbara how she would feel about visiting with other members of our group who were interested in healing, and she was delighted by the possibility. I made arrangements to call her the next day to finalize the meeting time and place, which would have to be in the city, rather than in her apartment.

As Jai and I moved to the door, I felt we were leaving a very old and dear friend. Our hugs and wispy tears confirmed the heartfelt connection we had made. Clutching the precious manuscripts in one hand, I took Jai's hand in the other as we heard the chain again being fastened in our wake. We ambled silently down the gloomy hall, made our way to the stairs, walked down a flight and pushed the elevator button. The babushka-informer in the lobby was gone. We pushed through the doors back onto the cold street, where the people were continuing in their self-possessed way to walk the well worn routes between the buildings.

I felt a sense of sadness coupled with joy. The contrast between the outer and inner worlds of the Soviets was evident. I felt saddened by the obvious tragedies and heartened by the connection I had shared with Barbara. It was as though the pressure from the external realities imposed by the state had forced the people inside, to develop a depth of heart and soul that I had never before experienced.

I breathed in and accepted my sadness, and began to transform it into commitment. I would honor Barbara by publishing her writings. I would help her see her dream come true. It would be one more small contribution toward people-to-people communication and citizen diplomacy.

■ II.

The Soviet Psychic Healing Controversy

The person to go down in history is not the one who first discovers something but the one who first has the courage to admit it.

Wieslaw Brudzinski

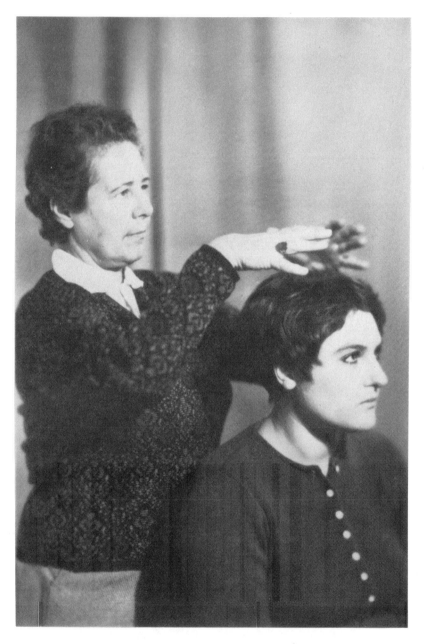

Barbara Ivanova performing a healing

According to Yet Unknown Laws of Nature

Despite reports that official support is given to Soviet healers, in fact the subject remains a controversial one among official circles.* In the influential Academy of Sciences of the USSR, for example, debate continues about the validity and value of research into "biofield influence," and numerous articles have been published on the discussions.

In considering the Soviet psychic healing controversy, we provide an informational context for Barbara Ivanova's work. Our first selection, *According to Yet Unknown Laws of Nature*, includes excerpts from an exemplary "Round Table" discussion with healers in Moscow, followed by an interview with Barbara which was published in a Yugoslavian magazine.

The article contains excerpts from the April 1981 (No. 17) issue of the Soviet magazine, *Ogonyek*. One year earlier the magazine had invited a number of healers, scientists, engineers, and physicians to Moscow for a discussion of several questions: What is the biofield of a human being? Are there proofs for its existence? Can one person influence another person by his bioenergy? Do/should scientists investigate such phenomena?

The healers included Djuna Davitashvili, Viktor Krivorotov, Georgi Kenchadze and Barbara Ivanova. It is particularly interesting that the editors of *Ogonyek* chose the title of their article from the speech given by Barbara at the discussion.—Eds.

Moderator: Today we will discuss problems about which many people have rather skeptical attitudes. Psychotronics is a new trend in science which studies the reserves and possibilities of man, as well as his bioenergetics and distant interactions with other objects and subjects.

---

* Western research in "psychic" healing has been summarized in the article by Dr. Jerry Solfvin, "Mental Healing," in *Advances in Parapsychological Research* (Dr. Stanley Krippner, Ed.), Vol. 4, Jefferson, N.C.: McFarland, 1984.—Eds.

We have as our guest Djuna Davitashvili, about whom much has been written and argued in our press. Of course, Djuna is not the only extrasenser. According to very approximate estimations, there are about two hundred such people in Moscow alone. They all possess, to differing degrees, increased sensitivity to the biofield of other people, and the ability to influence it. Those who encounter the phenomenon for the first time view it as a miracle.

D. Davitashvili: Of course, there is no miracle here. There is a biological field around all living organisms, including human beings, which we extrasensers feel very easily. This biofield changes depending on physical and even psychical states of the organism. Therefore, when I pass my hands along the patient's body, I can tell at once which organs of the body are diseased. Various diseases cause different sensations in my hands, such as prickling, warmth or other sensations not easy to define.

The energy system of our body has many outlets on the skin; they have been known for thousands of years as so-called acupuncture points. Physicians who treat by means of acupuncture activate the defense forces of the organism and thus help the fight against disease. I think that we do the same. We influence the active points of the energy system of a person and enhance the restorative processes.

I would like to add that such an influence is impossible without a favorable attitude toward the person. Without it the influence of the extrasenser on the person will be inefficient. A healer has to be a kind person who loves people.

If we learn to control the bioenergetics of the organism, it will not be necessary to treat diseases. We will simply be able to prevent them from occurring. Although this is a task for the future, we must today apply as much effort as possible to solve the mysteries of the human body, about which we yet know very little.

Moderator: Several days ago at our editorial office, the extrasensers Victor Krivorotov, Evgeny Dubitsky, Pavel Sokolov, and Nikolai Troyan demonstrated their abilities to diagnose and relieve the pain of patients suffering with radiculitis (sciatica). The physicians present were extremely surprised. They were amazed both by the disappearance and relief of the pains, and the very fact of bioenergy influence—that this is not magic, nor sorcery, nor trickery of charlatans. It is a pity that our experiments were so short.

Numerous attempts have been made to investigate biofield influence, including experiments at the polyclinic of the State Planning Committee with Djuna Davitashvili. But Irina Petrovna Chekmacheva, the chief physician of the polyclinic of the USSR State Planning Committee, is better qualified to talk about this research.

I. Chekmacheva: We attempted to treat, by biofield influence, patients suffering from acute diseases of the autonomic nervous system: acute radiculitis (sciatica) and osteochondritis of the spinal column. A pronounced pain syndrome and limitations in movement of the extremities were observed in all patients before treatment. The pain decreased after the very first session. After the fifth session, the pain was totally relieved in all patients, and full use of the extremities was restored. I cannot say whether this recovery is complete, as it is necessary to wait for some time. But it is possible to affirm with confidence that Djuna has an obvious ability to influence the course of disease.

We also conducted a functional examination of the patients by means of special equipment. The devices showed that after seven or eight sessions the condition of the vascular system of the head and extremities was improved, and that the blood circulation and arterial and venous tone had normalized. Heart activity and the condition of the digestive system had also improved.

Of course, the research conducted is clearly insufficient. It is necessary to continue the work and to invite various specialists to participate in it.

Moderator: Recently, similar investigations were conducted at the Moscow Polyclinic No. 36 under the direction of V.I. Vashkevich, head of the consultative and diagnostic center of the Frunzensky region of the city. For six weeks Djuna Davitashvili conducted diagnoses of several dozen patients who had been previously examined in medical institutions. The clinical diagnosis and the determination of the disease by the extrasenser have coincided in more than ninety-seven percent of cases. Moreover, Djuna revealed other diseases in half of the patients, later confirmed in most cases by clinical examination.

An interesting experiment, in which Djuna Davitashvili participated, was conducted at the Institute of Reflex Therapy. Its aim was to record the action of the extrasenser upon the patient's organism by means of such sensitive devices as the heat detector. The device showed an increase in the hand temperature of the patient (who was suffering from a disorder of vascular circulation in the extremities) after the influence of the extrasenser.

Unfortunately, the research has been discontinued.

And one more interesting fact: some physicians told me that Djuna helped them to develop their abilities of bioenergy influence.

D. Davitashvili: Yes, I helped to reveal such possibilities to the physician-oncologist I. Nadzharova, gynecologist D. Eristani, E. Dubitsky and others. Each person can master such an ability, in the same way that everyone can learn to play piano, but not everyone will become a Beethoven. It is not necessary to teach this ability to everyone, but only to physicians.

Moderator: Research has been conducted in our country for some time. As early as fifteen years ago, the Laboratory for Bioinformation was established at the Popov Society. A teacher, Barbara Mikhailovna Ivanova, at present a member of the International Association for Psychotronic Research, took an active role in its work.

B. Ivanova: At that time our research was headed by Professor I.M. Kogan. When he argued with skeptics (which he did frequently), he liked to quote D.I. Mendeleev, who is widely known for his work in little-understood phenomena. Some time ago Mendeleev headed the commission for research of parapsychological phenomena. He said these phenomena "should not be disregarded, but rather considered, that is, as to whether they belong to presently unexplained phenomena which occur *according to yet unknown laws of nature.*"

The phenomena about which we speak today could possibly occur according to yet unknown laws of nature. What law known to us can explain that plant seeds, subjected to the bioinfluence of the extrasenser Nina Sergeyevna Kulagina, grow more rapidly than plants from control seeds? And what law can explain the experiments of Estonian scientist T. Neeme, who proved that it is possible to increase the speed of sedimentation in solutions treated by human bioenergy? If we do not know these laws, does it mean that we have to deny the very phenomena as non-existent?

L. Sukharebsky, M.D., Director of the Institute of Uvenology (the Soviet term for the field studying physical immortality): For my whole life I have been involved with our topic of discussion today. I have thought much about these phenomena and I believe that attitudes to them will change in the near future. Reserves of the human organism are inexhaustible, but do we know them and how to use them? Science postulates that a human being uses seven to eight percent of his creative potential. Recently, a hypothesis appeared which considered that the human brain has a so-called "second bottom" and that a person can live his whole life without discovering this second bottom. I, as an experienced psychiatrist, can say the following: the essence of the influence we are talking about today is the human ability to mobilize brain reserves in the person whom we try to help.

N. Nikolayeva, member of the Presidium of the International Association for Psychotronic Research: Seven years ago four well-known psychologists published an article entitled: "Parapsychology: Fiction or Reality?" in the journal *Questions of Philosophy*. The article evoked great interest, primarily because it recognized, after much discussion, some so-called parapsychological phenomena. Seven years have passed, and we are still at the same level. We are still trying to prove to each other that this is "not fiction, but reality," and that obviously "there is something in it." This situation will continue until we understand that this is a social problem of contemporary human beings living in the epoch of scientific and technological revolutions and "information explosions." The methods of diagnosis and healing we speak about today were known three thousand years ago in ancient India, Tibet and other countries. Today, scientists of the whole world often speak about the necessity of using the wisdom of ancient teachings in contemporary medicine. Bridges have to be constructed between medicine of the West and of the East in the course of studying man and his possibilities.

Moderator: It is interesting to know how the matter stands with foreign researchers. Eduard Konstantinovich Naumov, associate member of the International Parapsychological Association, will tell us about this.

E. Naumov: At present, parapsychological research is going on in more than thirty-five countries of the world. According to official data, there are more than 250 organizations in the world which are engaged in studies of the problem. International congresses, seminars, and symposia are conducted regularly. Scientists who work in the fields of psychology, cybernetics, and electronics are interested more and more in research in this area. Interesting results have been obtained in telepathy, remote viewing, and in studying so-called altered states of consciousness. For example, there are intriguing experiments in inducing dreams by suggesting certain information to a sleeping person.

Moderator: It would be incorrect to say that the phenomena we discuss today are not studied in our country. Among the first scientists to study these mysterious phenomena was Victor Adamenko, who defended the initial thesis on the Kirlian effect in this country. Today he takes part in our meeting.

V. Adamenko: About twenty years ago I began to work with the Kirlians. The Kirlians studied processes on the skin of a human being and on the surface of plant leaves. They were the first to obtain pictures of the finger radiations of Alexei Krivorotov and his patients, finding the difference in pictures before and after the healer's influence. The selfless thirty year work of the inventors has been highly appreciated by scientists of many countries, and now the method of photographing life systems by means of high frequency discharge is known as Kirlian photography all over the world.

I was primarily interested in the physical mechanism of the formation of radiation emitted from living organisms. Kirlian photographs register this radiation by means of high frequency electrical discharges. As a result of many years of research, I have managed to prove the electronic nature of this radiation. A Kirlian "picture" is a biofield pattern. However, the most interesting point is that these pictures change, depending on the condition of the organism. For example, their brightness and color often depend on the emotional state of a person. These changes have attracted the attention of psychologists, physicians, and biologists to Kirlian photography. Today, there are institutes abroad which study the Kirlian method.

It is a pity that such an interesting phenomenon, which was discovered in our country, is virtually unstudied here.

Moderator: I recently visited Alma-Ata, where interesting studies of the biofield are carried out at the Division of Biophysics of Kazakh State University, headed by the Doctor of Biological Sciences, Professor Victor Mikhailovich Inyushin. For the first time, they have obtained photographs of natural radiations emitted by living objects (without optic systems and without any high frequency discharges). This fact nonplused many scientists, since it is impossible from the point of view of today's knowledge.

Victor Inyushin put forward an interesting hypothesis: his idea is that the material essence of the biological field of a living organism is bioplasma; that is, the stable complex of elementary particles. According to Inyushin, the bioplasma is a carrier of the organism's bioenergy.

At present, the Alma-Ata biophysicists intend to conduct some sophisticated experiments in transmission of energy from one biological object to another. This transfer of energy is supposed to be implemented by means of a special resonator and lasers.

As you see, there are many ideas, thoughts and hypotheses, and now the most important point is to unite and direct them in the most appropriate way. However, one must not forget that unfortunately there are many charlatans who claim to have unique abilities, as well as many non-competent specialists, and also simply fans of sensationalism and fashionable interests. It is important to separate the false from the genuine.

This idea is not new. As writer Leonid Leonov stated that Maxim Gorky once told him, "We should build a special institute, gather there folk healers, sorcerers, and other people of such a kind, and let them... share their mysteries and secrets of nature which they managed to come to know. Not all of them are rogues —there are also very talented people, sharp-sighted and perspicacious."

Speaking about this, Leonid Leonov added, "Much has already been missed, but it is necessary to reap a harvest from these extraordinary people before it is too late."

Participants of the Round Table in Moscow

A Letter from
Barbara Ivanova

In the following letter, Barbara elaborates on the discrepancy between official publications and the reality of the situation for healers in the Soviet Union. She explains the experiments conducted prior to the Round Table discussion, and considers the difficulties of experimenter bias in official laboratory research. In conclusion, she notes that the controversy between the official position and that of independent parapsychologists was aggravated by the preceding *Ogonyek* article, and that the situation worsened for healers following its publication. —Eds.

Dear Friends,

This letter is to explain the real events concerning our Round Table meeting which was described in the article in *Ogonyek*, published in April, 1981. First of all—the meeting occurred exactly a year earlier. It was planned contrary to the way it appeared, and it happened not as described. However, positive persons attempted, as best they could, to publish at least a part of the real truth.

A day before the Round Table, a series of experiments were carried out in a clinic, under strict control. The best healers of the country were gathered, but no positive results were registered— not even one. Since we were invited, most of us had two feelings: we were glad that at least there were official experiments, and yet we were nervous because we suspected something behind it.

When we saw that our efforts showed no measurable changes, at first we could not understand it. The normalization of blood pressure, for example, can be achieved by each of my students after two days of learning. And there were no cases which registered it, even after the work of a dozen of the best healers! It simply could not be true. Later we understood the reasons. I will not explain them fully now, but I would like to mention a very important fact: when I helped a woman before the official experiments began, and she registered the changes in her blood pressure herself (not the

43

persons who were responsible for the tests that day), there were good results: from 170/95 to 120/80 in one minute! I cannot say that my abilities are better than that of all the others. And in any case it would not explain why I could not repeat the same result in further tests, controlled by the official persons, and why I **do** repeat it many times during my other experiments, and have over many years.

I talked about this in my brief speech at the Round Table (where I was placed together with four other healers—Krivorotov [the son], Kenchadze, Safonov, and Djuna Davitashvili; Djuna was one of us—as an equal, not as the only healer as was published). There were other individuals as well—from the administration, the organizers, scientists, and a representative from the State Committee for Science and Technology (Medical Department). We answered questions from the people present, described our work, and showed what we could do—all of us. The press conference lasted for five hours, although only a small portion was published.

At the conference, results obtained by all of us (healers) were described by participants of other experiments. Among them there were cases of several persons who had helped to close wounds (mastitis), to rapidly heal ulcers, to relieve headaches, and to heal skin diseases, as well as my own distant (telephone contact) healing. I regret that this information was not published.

I also conducted an experiment in demonstrating to the audience how they could feel and activate their own radiations. This also was not mentioned in the publication, despite the fact that two-thirds of the audience felt their own energy field, received the necessary feedback, and reported it.

There was another point in my speech which I wish to reiterate: I said that if one has the ability to radiate bioenergy, it is not enough to give one the right to heal. First of all, a harmonization of both, patient and healer, is necessary, and only afterwards may one try to send his energy. Also, there can be no lasting results without a certain ethical and moral level. This is a law of Nature and the main principle in healing. It is a pity that they did not publish this vital point.

In any case, however, the fact that such a publication appeared has some intriguing implications, with all its complications and controversies. But, regrettably, this does not mean a reconciliation between the official point of view and our work and the activities of independent parapsychologists (on the contrary—after this publication many things got worse). The fight for our science of parapsychology is proceeding still, and we all work toward a positive parapsychology, an open one—that is, not hidden behind walls and doors.

I hope you understood my main points. Wishing you much luck in your work,

Yours sincerely,

Barbara Ivanova
June 1981

Thus, it is obvious from the above letter that in spite of a considerable increase of interest in psychic healing in the Soviet Union, there exists a difficult situation for many healers there. Perhaps some readers might consider Barbara Ivanova's statement that psychic healing sessions are unsuccessful in the presence of negatively-minded individuals as non-scientific. Yet this outcome may be probable in light of the existing data on biofield interactions between individuals such as the experimenter effect in ESP tests (i.e., that an experimenter's attitude might influence the outcome of the experiment). Nevertheless, the more open we are to these new ideas, the quicker we will find solutions for many unexplored mysteries of nature.—Eds.

The Healing Results of Barbara Ivanova

As mentioned previously, the "official" experiments conducted in conjunction with the Soviet Round Table discussion did not yield substantive results. In contrast, the following statements indeed attest to the efficacy of Barbara's healing influence. — Eds.

Statement No. 1

Six days before a lecture of B. Ivanova I burned my left hand with boiling water and unfortunately stripped off the blister. By the sixth day the scar was violet in color and looked terrible.

During her lecture Ivanova said, "Everybody who feels physical pains or mental discomfort, please raise your hands and turn your palms to me." I raised my hands, forgetting about my burn and thinking about an almost nonexistent headache. I wanted very much that the headache should immediately disappear, but it was invented and did not change.

When we left the lecture hall, a woman looked at my burned hand with sympathy, and I said, "Perhaps, somebody can heal it." I came home and the next morning noticed that the skin on my burned hand became young and pink (previously it was wrinkled and violet). The next day my acquaintances looked at my healed hand and found it startling.

N. Kryukova,
Teacher in Music
Moscow

Statement No. 2

I am very grateful to Barbara Ivanova for giving me five sessions of healing when I asked her to help me because I had pneumonia.

On the morning of October 8, an X-ray examination showed that I had pneumonia (inflammation in the right lung). My temper-

ature was 37.8°C (the normal temperature is 37.0°C). On the evening of October 9, having a temperature of 38.3°C, I turned to
Barbara by phone, asking her to help me (I am seventy-eight years
old). Barbara immediately gave me the first session of healing at a
distance, speaking to me by phone. In the morning of October 10
I felt well; my temperature was 37.3°C. In the evening it was 37.2°C,
and continued to decrease, not exceeding the norm.

On October 12 a physician from the polyclinic who visited me
did not detect inflammation in my lung.

On October 13 Barbara gave me the last session. During one
session she relieved a headache which I did not feel any more
afterwards. At present I feel well and in good spirits.

Elena V.*
Moscow,
November 18, 1978*

Statement No. 3

I am a student, thirty years old. While with Barbara Ivanova, I
occasionally touched my right leg and after feeling pain and swelling of the size of a two kopek (one cent) coin, remembered that I
had hurt myself earlier that day. I told Barbara about my pain.
Without turning to me she answered, "One moment," and began
to concentrate. In about half a minute the pain almost disappeared,
and I told Barbara about this. Barbara, hearing that a slight pain
remained, said, "I will try a little bit more." In about half a minute
I felt that the whole area on my leg about the size of my palm
became numb as if I had a local anesthesia. The swelling also
disappeared. I was very surprised that in only one minute Barbara
could eliminate both pain and swelling which I did not feel again.

Signature withheld
Moscow

Statement No. 4

In the fall of 1982 I had been suffering from severe backaches

---

*Some of Barbara's patients asked her not to publicize their names. Dates are
indicated where known. — Eds.

(sciatica) for two months. For days I could not get out of bed. During this time I was receiving various kinds of medical treatment (drugs, physiotherapy, vitamins, massage, etc.). However, nothing seemed to relieve the pain. My cousin advised me to consult with Barbara Ivanova. In January 1983, I attended one of Barbara's lectures and after the lecture I asked her for help. Before working with me, she worked with a woman who suffered from hypertension and severe headaches. After seven to ten minutes of Barbara's treatment, the woman said her headache disappeared completely and that she felt well. Afterwards she began working with me. I was wearing a heavy coat and asked Barbara if I should take it off. She answered that this was unnecessary. Interestingly, during the healing session I felt pleasant warmth coming to me through my coat. In five to ten minutes (I was not aware of the exact time) the session ended. To my surprise, immediately after the session I felt no pain and was able to bend forward and touch the floor with my hands. I was truly astonished.

> Taisiya Razmyslovich
> Moscow
> September 30, 1976

Statement No. 5

I had a bad infection on my finger which needed lancing. I made an appointment with my doctor to lance it on August 21, 1980. I tried various folk and medical remedies, including applying aloe vera, hot salt solutions, and ointments. My finger was hot, swollen, painful to the touch, and would not bend.

On August 20 Barbara Ivanova held her left hand over my infected finger and promised that the pus underneath my nail would begin to exude. That's exactly what happened. The next morning I found that my bandage had absorbed all the pus. The infection healed entirely, and when I went to my doctor's appointment the following day, the doctor wasn't able to understand why I didn't need the lancing.

> Svetlana
> Moscow
> August 25, 1980

Statement No. 6

I had a bad toothache due to an abscess which caused a large swelling on my right cheek and neck. I had an appointment with the dentist the next morning. The evening before, a friend of mine, Galina, came to my house. I went downstairs to meet her and told her about my toothache. A woman whom I did not know was with Galina in her car (I later learned that she was Barbara Ivanova). She expressed an interest in helping me. She got out of the car and moved her hands several times around my head. I was very skeptical about the results, but expressed my gratitude to her. However, the next morning the toothache and the swelling on my face and neck were completely gone.

Prof. A.P. Yufin
Doctor in Engineering
Moscow

Psychic Healing Can Be Learned

(An Interview with Barbara Ivanova)

Throughout 1981 a Yugoslavian magazine, *Vikend* (Weekend), published a series of articles about Barbara Ivanova and psychic healing in the USSR, written by A. Bele after his visit to the Soviet Union. These include "General Psi Healing through Telephone," No. 683, June 26, 1981; "(Un)disclosed Riddle of Barbara Ivanova," No. 691, August 21, 1981 and "Psychic Healing Can be Learned," No. 693, September 4, 1981. The first two articles describe Barbara's research results and activities, with a special emphasis on her results in distant (remote) healing. Included, for example, are her treatments of patients in Novosibirsk (at a distance of 2,000 kilometers), and in Yugoslavia while speaking to them by telephone from Moscow. The article below is an abridged translation from *Vikend* of September 4, 1981 which describes an interview with Barbara. — Eds.

■ Barbara Ivanova believes that most people, regardless of their age and sex, can become healers. According to her, however, extroverts have better chances of mastering healing abilities than introverts.

"Can I become a healer?" I asked Barbara Ivanova during our conversation in Moscow.

She did not seem surprised by this question and answered, "One has to fulfill some preliminary conditions."

Vikend: "What are the conditions?"

Barbara: "A person has to know psychology and, to a certain extent, parapsychology. He/she has to be fair and eager to help people. This means that a healer cannot and should not be egotistical."

Vikend: "There were rumors that one of the Soviet mediums, Nina Kulagina, using psychotronic energy (the influence of mind over matter) destroyed the American atomic submarine *Thresher*. Do you know whether this is true?"

Barbara: "I know nothing about this but I think that under certain conditions psi forces could have destructive capabilities beyond that of atomic weaponry. The nature of psi has not been sufficiently studied to know to what extent it can be used for negative purposes."

Vikend: "How do you teach people to be healers?"

Barbara: "There are roughly three stages. During the first stage students become acquainted with the subject and the necessary literature. Relaxation, meditation, and the induction of their abilities follow. At the same time, using my bioenergy, I try to activate the bioenergy of my students. Some of the students sense the influence of my bioenergy as heat; some of them receive an impression that the room becomes lighter; some sense the smell of ozone. Obviously, there are individual differences in perceiving the same phenomenon."

Vikend: "How long does it take to become a healer?"

Barbara: "It depends on the person; usually not less than one year."*

Perhaps readers think that these descriptions of psychic healing are very strange. However, according to Barbara Ivanova, there is nothing strange in this method. Barbara expresses this as follows, "The healing that I perform results from the influence of bioenergy. We know that everyone radiates this kind of energy, and healers possess it to a greater degree. During our sessions, this energy transforms into a force which heals the disease. You can judge what the possibilities are from the fact that I can stop bleeding from a wound within twenty seconds."

One can believe that these phenomena occur due to the ability of all living organisms to radiate and perceive gravitation waves, according to the hypothesis of Alexander Dubrov. His theory suggests that a person can influence the environment with this energy.

---

* Barbara believes that some individuals who are already at a high level of spiritual development, may learn to become good healers in less than one year.

Development of Abilities of Remote Diagnosis and Psychic Healing: Methodology and Research Results Obtained by Barbara Ivanova

Larissa Vilenskaya

■ My close friend and colleague Barbara Ivanova began her work in the field of healing in 1971, developing her own abilities of healing (bioenergy influence) and later those of her students. Barbara has done much to spread interest and information about psychic healing and psi in general in the Soviet Union. Her numerous talks, lectures, and workshops in various cities and towns throughout the USSR revealed the intriguing world of psi for millions of people and helped many of them to discover healing capacities in themselves. Barbara arrived at the bold idea, "Everyone can learn to heal!" She was the first who began using telephone contact during healing sessions with the view that an individual's voice is as unique as his/her photograph and helps the healer to tune in and strengthen contact with the patient. And she has been very insistent upon providing evidence for these ideas.

Barbara's first attempt to research the subject was carried out within the framework of the Seminar on Bioelectronics and subsequently at the Laboratory for Bioinformation at the A.S. Popov Scientific and Technological Society for Radioelectronics and Communication. There she headed an experimental and training group (1973–1975). At the same time she began to work in studying mass psychoregulation and healing influence. She has delivered many lectures on the subject, promoted understanding and acceptance of the method, and has trained hundreds of healers throughout the country.

In her experimental and training work, Barbara Ivanova set the following goals:[1]

1. General personality harmonizing of the participants;
2. Heightening their creative potential;
3. Obtaining healing results (on mind and body);
4. Strengthening the person (psychologically and physiologically) against possible stress, diseases, etc.;
5. Training the ability to control the functions and dysfunctions of the body;
6. Cultivating certain psycho-physiological reactions, needed in life, in work, with friends, with colleagues, in the family, etc.

In the general harmonizing, educating and healing work, Barbara has been using three main types of processes:

1. Direct transference of harmonizing, vitalizing, and healing radiations from the experimenter (healer) to an individual or to the whole audience;
2. Attaining a special state of mind and body in the audience by some collective meditation-related immersion exercises, connected with auto-immersions, into slightly altered states of consciousness and body conditions appropriate for self-harmonizing, self-educating, self-healing, etc.;
3. Creation (and/or activation) of a mutual energy-field, which makes possible a unified, mutually positive influence between the participants, with vitalizing, harmonizing, healing and other results.

In the process of this work Barbara achieved the following results:

A) *Physiological Results:*

1. Normalization of blood pressure;
2. Dissolution of calcium in bones and vessels;
3. Amelioration of general heart and vessel conditions;
4. Decrease or even disappearance of certain tumors—sometimes immediately;
5. Cessation of hemorrhages (as yet only of small wounds);
6. Rapid healing of small wounds;
7. Relieving almost any type of pain. Generally the cause disappears along with the pain; the effect lasts hours, days, or years;
8. Rehabilitation of patients with certain types of ulcers.

B) *Psychological Results:*

1. Relief from effects of stress, nervousness, insomnia, restlessness, etc.;
2. General harmony, equilibrium, calmness, and mental stability;
3. Development of different kinds of creativity;
4. Increase of energy, an ability to study or to work, better results in various lines of activity;
5. Outbursts of optimism, will to live, to work, to be active;
6. Minutes of happiness, sometimes even euphoria (in some cases the duration of the effect is longer).

C) *Educative (Social) Results*

1. Positive shift in the attitude of the person toward facts, situations, persons, etc.; personal and family relations improving as the result of this, problems solved easier, work going better, social stress-situations lessening, etc.;
2. Positive changes in the whole personality—in one's general orientation, interests, activities, behavior, contacts, manners, etc.;
3. Rehabilitation of alcoholics, excessive smokers, etc.

In general, the results obtained have been as follows: sixty to eighty percent of the pains, discomforts, negative attitudes, vices, and other symptoms of disharmony in mind and body disappear along with the illnesses and other factors which caused the disharmonies. All this varies, depending on the person, the purpose of the group, the audience, the place, etc. For example: in Moscow, for almost any audience, the healing results were not more than sixty to seventy percent of the ailment-cases. In Leningrad they were eighty to ninety percent. In Sukhumi (Caucausus) and in Novgorod, ninety to one hundred percent. The same percentages occurred with the experiments in clairvoyant diagnosis. In the latter cities, traditional (folk) healing practices have been widely practiced and accepted for centuries.

Subjectively healing energies irradiated by Barbara during healing treatments are often felt by patients as sensations of heat or cold, prickling, and tingling. The most interesting fact is that the involvement of suggestion is quite unlikely here because many patients report such sensations spontaneously, having never heard about them and never having been told to expect them.

The results in healing and psychoregulation achieved by Barbara Ivanova have been studied at clinics and other medical institutions in the USSR.* Below are extracts from documents which were given to her in 1976, after a series of experiments with healing (bioenergy stimulation) on some forms of harmonizing and vitalizing influences, which were verified by medical means:

Before the treatment:	After the treatment:	Remarks:
1. Blood pressure (BP) 180/100, headache	BP 120/80, no complaints	distance— 10 miles one session
2. BP 90/60, weakness	BP 110/70, energy, happiness	one session
3. BP 160/100, nervousness, giddiness, etc.	BP 120/80, feeling well	distance— 1 meter, one session
4. benign tumor on right leg, 3 x 2 cm.	1.5 x 1 cm.	one session
5. benign tumor near left ear, 3 x 1.5 cm.	1 x 0.5 cm.	one session
6. thrombosis; a thrombus on left hand, 4 x 1 cm., pains	thrombus dissolved; no pains; thrombosis-index reduced to 85%	four sessions
7. a bad drunkard and smoker; family destroyed, health weak, complexion pale	no more wish to drink or to smoke, and aversion to it; family, mood and health re-established; happy, well	four sessions
8. puberty-age psychosteny; psychotic, asocial, etc.	less aggressive, more calm; began to speak and to eat together with family, etc.	five sessions
9. antritis (sinusitis); could scarcely breathe, pains.	began to breathe normally; less complaints.	five sessions

---

* The names of the institutions are not indicated due to the difficulties which may be caused by an unauthorized publication abroad.—Eds.

■ As is widely known, the issue of development of psi ability is very controversial. Some researchers believe that the cultivation of these abilities, i.e., the implementation of a process of learning, is quite possible. Others think that a majority of the existing methods intended to develop ESP, PK, and/or psychic healing abilities are only capable of eliminating the psychological obstacles of subjects and thus increasing their performance in experiments. Foregoing a detailed discussion of this controversy and referring readers to the extensive work by Dr. Jeffrey Mishlove,[2] I would like to describe briefly some training methods developed by Barbara Ivanova. Her method of training of clairvoyant diagnosis enabled her numerous students to identify various disorders of the organism, as well as locations of scars, traces of former fractures, operations, etc. (under clothing and when a person was at some distance from the experimenter, even at a distance of dozens of kilometers).

In one of her publications,[3] Barbara partially explained her method for increasing the perception of intuitive information (in her terminology). She stated that during a group training session the leader of the group gave the students instructions as follows:

1. Imagine some pleasant event or any picture or image which pleases you.
2. Try to understand and remember how you have imagined this—what place this mental image occupied in your mind.
3. "Wipe off" from your "inner screen" everything that you imagined and create a vacuum in your mind (in Barbara's opinion, this would mean a readiness to passive reception).
4. When the experimenter gives a task-program (e.g., to identify the location of a scar on the body of a person situated in another room), wait passively until an image fills the vacuum. In other words, wait for the appearance of quasi-visual or quasi-auditory images in the same way and in the same place of your mind where you previously had a conscious positive image.

Using group relaxation and various exercises on visualization of spontaneous and programmed images, in addition to the above procedure, Barbara indicated that after several training sessions, many of her students were able to perform remote diagnosis and successfully determine the nature and location of diseases, as well as locations of pains, scars, tumors, etc. The most gifted students sometimes could receive the name of a disease in medical terms, as quasi-auditory information, while not possessing knowledge of medicine and in some cases not even understanding what this name meant. More often students gave some features and locations of disorders of the human body, without giving the exact name of the disease.

According to Barbara Ivanova, the same method also leads to the development of the ability to perceive general intuitive (i.e., clairvoyant, including precognitive) information, not necessarily connected with medical problems. Possessing these abilities herself, she observed that the results of the training group were much higher when training sessions were conducted by a psychic person. Thus, it appears that not only the training method itself is important but rather some kind of psychic (wordless) influence of a group leader. Furthermore, Barbara used, in the process of training, special *mediumistic texts,* where both content and forms of pronunciation are important: intonation, voice-modulation, rhythm, and stress. A most interesting feature is that she received these texts in an intuitive way, without a conscious knowledge of which intonation and rhythm were necessary.

Barbara also observed that her collective relaxation sessions, in addition to enhancing results of tests in receiving intuitive information, relieve tiredness and anxiety in many participants, as well as alleviate some pains and disorders.[3] It should be noted that Barbara started her work in intuitive diagnosis after several years of activities in development and successful application of psychic healing (bioenergy stimulation, in her terminology).[1,3-7]

It is extremely interesting that when comparing approaches and results of various psychic healers, one will find more similarities than differences even if these healers live in different countries and have never heard about each other. Some time ago I was fortunate (thanks to Dr. Jeffrey Mishlove) to observe some healing sessions of a Brazilian healer (Brother Macedo). Without considering to what extent his results are caused by psychotherapy and to what extent psychic healing, i.e., bioenergy therapy (for such consideration see, for example, an article by the Soviet healer Krivorotov[8]), I would like to indicate some common features of the healers' methods. Both of them are able to perform mass sessions of healing (Barbara Ivanova—during her lectures, and Brother Macedo—during mutual meditations of participants). Neither need to know the exact medical diagnosis to perform healing, believing that their radiations will find the diseased organ or system (weak spots) in the patient's body. At the same time, Brother Macedo discovered his healing powers spontaneously, while Barbara, being a researcher, developed her abilities and continues to develop and enhance them. Nevertheless, the "telergy" (as he coined it), applied by Brother Macedo, and the bioenergy applied by Soviet healers, are, in my opinion, manifestations of the same process of interaction of human beings which is as yet not understood by science.

Perhaps the results of Barbara's studies will extend the application of psi in everyday life. They may also confirm the viewpoint expressed recently by psychologist Keith Harary[9] that psi possibly does not transcend space and time, but rather our *concepts* of space and time, based on contemporary limited knowledge.

References

1. Ivanova, B. "Experimental and Training Work on Some Group (Mass) Harmonizing Processes with Educating, Creativity-Heightening and Healing Results," *Proceedings of Second International Congress on Psychotronic Research*, Tokyo, 1977, pp. 463-471.

2. Mishlove, J. *Psi Development Systems.* Jefferson, N.C., & London: McFraland, 1983.

3. Ivanova, B. "Intuitive Forecasting (Experimental and Training Work)," *Proceedings of Second International Congress on Psychotronic Research.* Monte Carlo, 1975, pp. 322-325.

4. Ivanova, B. "Guarizioni a distanza," *Metapsichica* (Rivista Italiana di Parapsicologia), Anno XXIX, Fasc. I-II, Gennanio-Giugno 1974, pp. 28-32.

5. Ivanova, B. "Psycho- and Auto-Regulation," *International Journal of Paraphysics*, Vol. 12, Nos. 1/2, 1978, pp. 20-21.

6. Ivanova, B. "Cosmic Irradiations in (Mass) Healing Process: A Manifestation of Micro and Macro Cosmos Unity," *Proceedings of Fourth International Congress on Psychotronic Research*, São Paulo, Brazil, 1979, pp. 85-88.

7. Ivanova, B. "Integral Harmonizing, Healing and Other Kinds of Influence by Means of Psychoregulation, Autoregulation and Bioenergy Stimulation," *Parapsychology: Problems, Prospects, Possibilities (Proceedings of the First and Second Israeli Seminars on Parapsychology)*, L. Vilenskaya, (Ed.) (in press).

8. Krivorotov, V. "Some Issues of Bionergy Therapy," *Parapsychology in the USSR*, Part III, L. Vilenskaya (Ed.), San Francisco: Washington Research Center, 1981.

9. Harary, K. Personal communication, San Francisco, 1983.

Some Experiments on Healing Processes*

Barbara Ivanova

In the following selection, we see many facets of Barbara Ivanova: scientist, empiricist, logician, healer—working constantly to bridge the gaps between mind, body, and spirit.

She begins as a scientist, concerned with irradiation points, digital voltmeters, and oscillographs. In a breath, she is channeling cosmic energy and advocating positive thoughts of harmony, peace, and ethical elevation. Incessantly weaving a tapestry which includes colors of dynamic opposition, Barbara concludes, "The primary instrument for the investigation of the Universe is Man."—Eds.

■ Every biosystem has its innate laws of autoregulation. Our healing influence is like that of catalysts for natural processes. But moral factors play a much more important and basic role in the integral, true healing of Man.

There is no barrier between energy fields and the substance form of matter (e.g., the relationship of wave/particle in quantum mechanics). Energy is an inherent part of any biosystem. If a human body is drawn out of the energetic force field—as a result of actions, reactions, attitudes, etc.—the system gets holes, or defects in its energy counterpart which influence the body's substance and cause local points of disharmony or pathology. The simplest aspect of the task of a psychic healer is to serve as a channel, to activate and harmonize the interactive processes between living systems and the "energy ocean" to restore and correct the multicomponent fields. During 1977–80 experiments to verify the beneficial influence of a healer on another biosystem were conducted, in which my colleagues and I participated as organizers and healers. Three directions for these tests are briefly described below.

---

* The first version of the article was published in *Proceedings of the Fifth International Conference on Psychotronic Research*, Vol. 2, Bratislava, 1983.—Eds.

I. The late Dr. Veniamin Pushkin—an open-minded, serious researcher—worked on the methods for obtaining objective evidence of para-effects. Some of his lines of investigation[1] were almost simultaneously pursued by other researchers. Here is a description of one of these methods (as yet unpublished in the USSR):

a) In experiments carried out in Moscow, the subject, Dr. K. (who had a severe headache) was the receiver of energy and I was the donor or healer. The healing process was conducted with hand irradiations, twenty centimeters from the head of Dr. K., as well as with mental concentration from myself as the healer, without involving the hands.

Before the bioenergy influence, during it, and a minute after it, the electrical conductivity of some Biologically Active Points (BAPs) of the skin of both the healer and the subject were measured. For a measuring instrument we used the digital voltmeter "Shtch-1312." It gave us information about the bio-potentials. The influence of the healer (donor or inductor) on the subject (receiver) gave the following results: removal of headache, general well-being felt subjectively, and changes in the electrical conductivity measured objectively. The conductivity was almost one-third of its initial value and neared the normative zone of a healthy person in a good functional state. The healer generally feels tired after the experiments, and the conductivity of his BAPs rises. My value rose from 120 to 180—at the same active points where energy increased in the organism of the recipient. This leads to the conclusion that the healing proceeds through the flow of some type of energy from the healer to the subject (whose energy level rises, while it falls in the body of the healer).

b) In experiments conducted in the Physics section of the Moscow Society of Naturalists (headed by physicist Lev Druzhkin), we measured the electrical conductivity of the skin of some BAPs of the helix. This procedure was developed by a group of researchers,[2-4] and participating healers were engineer Vladimir Safonov and myself. My healing influence involved only mental concentration, without using my hands. Again, the points where our patients obtained a maximum of energy-rising showed loss of energy in the body of the healer.

II. Another method[5,6] was used in the laboratory of the USSR Academy of Sciences Research Institute of Evolutionary Morphology and Animal Ecology where the orientation of fish is being studied. A fish, *Gnathonemus petersii*, uses its own electrical field for orientation in the opacity of the Nile River water. Any object near it changes this field and the fish reacts. The impulses of its electrical organ, located in the tail, were recorded using a tape-recorder and an oscillograph.[*]

The electrical signals have a particular frequency when the fish is calm. But when we (parapsychologist Larissa Vilenskaya, myself, our students and other healers) put our hands near the aquarium (which was wrapped in an opaque material) and sent our impulses —the discharges of the fish were immediately much more frequent and energetic. When we ceased to send our energy—the frequency and the level of the reactions calmed down.

It is interesting to stress two variations of this effect: when the author channeled the Cosmic energy, using a special method (the *golden chalice*), the frequency and intensity level of impulses pro-duced by the fish was much higher than during the general activities of the other healers.[5] And when one of the experimenters (Olga Krug), after having excited the fish with her bare imagination, simply thought, "Be calm, I do not intend any harm"—the record-ing equipment showed that the fish became calmer.[6]

The doses of the irradiation quantity should be controlled: as with any type of medication, an increase of it may harm living systems. During our experiments we send energy for twenty to thirty seconds. The emission of our irradiations, connected with positive thoughts of harmony, peace, and ethical elevation brings eighty percent of the healing. We are very glad to be able to heal animals and plants as well.

But good results cannot be achieved in all cases. It depends on many factors, including personality traits, attitudes of the patient, the participants in the experiment, the state of the healer, karmic issues, and other important factors. An important hint to experi-menters: never expose fish and animals to many experiments at a time, or for a long duration. As with people it results in discomfort and pain. It is best to experiment at intervals of one to three hours, after the usual twenty to thirty second doses of psychic energy. A human being can say that he/she feels giddy, sick, etc.—and we stop the experiment immediately. That is why the author never

---

[*] See a detailed description of the procedure in the article by Vladimir Protasov, Lev Druzhkin, et al. "Nile Elephant *Gnathonemus petersii* as a Detector of External Influences" in *Doklady Akademii Nauk SSSR* (Reports of the USSR Academy of Sciences), vol. 260, No. 1, 1981. English translation of the article appeared in *Psi Research*, Vol. 2, No. 1, March 1983, pp. 31–37.—Eds.

heals without the possibility of verbal contact. If the healing is of the "out-of-sight" type or over large distances which we conduct frequently, there must be a telephone contact. But a so-called "dumb creature" (an animal, a pet, bird, or fish) cannot tell about its suffering—and we must be merciful.

The Cosmic contact which the author achieves with the golden chalice effect[5] and the soothing mental influence of the experimenter O. Krug[6] may easily be linked with the mass-harmonization work of the author[5,7] and distant healing experiments.[8,9]

III. The biolocation (dowsing) effect is another possible method to receive objective data on the healing bioenergy influence. We controlled the quantity of energy which was emitted during our series of experiments (carried out in 1980) from the healer (the author) to the recipient (Dr. Nikolai Sochevanov), under various conditions, during distant healing.[9]

Conclusion

Any technological method in psi research is only a part of the work. We need it because explanations in technical language—the language of numbers and formulae—is the only one which a certain mentality is able to understand (although, on the other hand, some scientists may argue that there have been not enough numbers and data presented in the article to allow proper evaluation of the experiments). However, the primary instrument for the investigation of the Universe is Man. In studying and explaining Man's capabilities we should not forget the main aspect: the *ethical laws*. Any infringement of them bears heavy consequences. The purely technological method leads to an impasse, and parapsychology must be controlled by ethical education—and by an international treaty, as in atomic weapons. *No science can exist without moral laws*—especially such a one that penetrates into the deep layers of the Micro and Macro Cosmos.

References

1. Nikiforov, V., Pushkin, V., Yermolayeva-Tomina, L., Shavyrina, G. "Information Energetics and the Problem of Psychological Fatigue in the Labor Process," in *VII Nauchno-tekhnicheskii seminar "Kontrol sostoyaniya cheloveka-operatora"* (Seventh Scientific-Technical Seminar "Control of the

State of Human Operator"), Annotations and Abstracts of Reports, Moscow, 1975, pp. 73–74 (in Russian).

2. Oksien, V. "On Research of Psychological Systems in Electrical High Frequency Fields," in *Voprosy psikhogigieny v sporte* (Questions of Psycho-Hygiene in Sport), Moscow: All-Union Research Institute of Physical Culture, 1975, pp. 126–137 (in Russian).

3. Oksien, V., Shkole, S. "Diagnosis of the State-Dynamics of Athletes with the Kirlian Effect," *Voprosy sportivnoi psikhologii* (Questions of Sport Psychology), Moscow: All-Union Research Institute of Physical Culture, 1975, pp. 94–97 (in Russian).

4. Alik, T. "Electro-Conductivity of Biologically Active Points of the Helix and Energy Interchange of the Organism in Pathological States and Nervous Mental Stresses," in V.I. Voitko & A.M. Korpukhina (Eds.), *Psikhofiziologicheskoe sostoyaniye cheloveka i informativnost biologicheski aktivnykh tochek kozhi* (Psychophysiological State of Individual and Informativeness of Biologically Active Points of the Skin), Kiev, 1979, pp. 9–11 (in Russian).

5. Ivanova, B. "Cosmic Irradiations in (Mass)-Healing Processes: Manifestation of Micro and Macro Cosmos Unity," in *Proceedings of the Fourth International Congress on Psychotronic Research*, São Paulo, 1979, pp. 85–88.

6. Editorial. "Little Nile-Elephant," *Znanie-Sila*, No. 9, 1979 (in Russian).

7. Ivanova, B. "Experimental and Training Work on Some Group Harmonizing Processes with Educational, Creativity-Heightening and Healing Results," in *Proceedings of the Third International Congress on Psychotronic Research*, Tokyo, 1977, pp. 463–471.

8. Pasian, R. "Fernheilung: zwischen UdSSR and USA" (Distant healing: Between the USSR and USA). *Esotera*, No. 6, 1974 (in German).

9. Ivanova, B. "The Biolocation Effect and Distant Influence of the Biofield," *Psi Research*, Vol. 2, No. 3, September 1983, pp. 9-20.

Barbara Ivanova and Vladimir Safonov, Soviet healers

■ III.

Transcending Contemporary Scientific Concepts

The limitation of Consciousness in space and time is such an overwhelming reality that every occasion when this fundamental truth is broken through must rank as an event of the highest theoretical significance, for it would prove that the space-time barrier can be annulled.

Carl Jung, *The Structure and Dynamics of the Psyche*

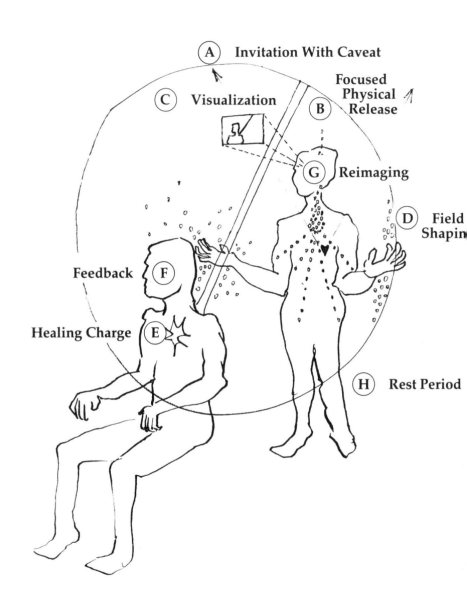

A graphic interpretaion of Barbara Ivanova's healing techniques

Rosa Kuleshova and Her Talent

Barbara Ivanova

In 1962, Rosa Kuleshova, from the city of Nizhny Tagil in the Ural mountains, not far from the cold plains of Soviet Siberia, was reported to have demonstrated the strange ability of "skin vision" or "dermo-optic" perception: being able to identify colors, drawings and even to read with her fingers. Rosa was subjected to numerous scientific tests and, after much controversy, her remarkable ability was confirmed. Barbara participated in some of these tests and was eager to share her impressions with our readers.

In January 1978, Rosa died suddenly in Sverdlovsk where she had lived during her last years. The officially announced cause of death was a hemorrhage associated with a brain tumor in the right occipital region. Since many people in the USSR do not believe official reports, there were other opinions concerning her death. Even if it was a result of the brain disease, some individuals believe that the real cause for Rosa's death was the continuous stress of the skepticism and mistrust of several of the researchers who conducted tests with her. — Eds.

■ Rosa Kuleshova is well known among parapsychologists throughout the world. After the publication of my article about Rosa Kuleshova in *The International Journal of Paraphysics* (Vol. 11, No. 1/2), I again had the opportunity to see demonstrations of her amazing abilities in dermo-optics (also called skin vision, cutaneous vision, or eyeless sight), but with added new skills she had developed.

In October 1977 the door-bell rang and Rosa entered, asking me to give her shelter in my home for several days. I had known that she was in Moscow to demonstrate her talent to the editorial staff of some journals because physicist Victor Adamenko had told me about it, and had asked me to help her by letting her stay in my flat for a few days. I naturally agreed! Now I wanted to gather an audience of experts, friends and colleagues, who had not seen her before, to give them the rare opportunity to see her demonstrations. Rosa could certainly persuade them that these are good proofs and real facts, rather than deserving the label, "charlatanism."

In the evening some open-minded, earnest friends arrived to see Rosa perform. The well-known Doctor of Physics and Mathematics, Professor Michael Romanovsky (author of comments to the article by Victor Adamenko on Kirlian photography—"The Lightning Takes Photographs" in *Nedelya*, No. 43, 1975) came with his son, a bright young physicist. Other guests included Mr. Stanislav Starikovich, an intelligent journalist, and engineer Valentina Tikhonova with her husband, also an engineer.

Soon, Rosa began her demonstration. This time, however, we slightly changed the method of her performance: the pages which she had to "read" with her fingertips, elbows, etc., were shielded not only from her sight, but from all of us, in order to rule out the possibility of a telepathic information-channel. One of us indicated the page for Rosa to read, without looking at the book. Another one called the number of the lines to be read. Rosa stood with her head covered and faced the wall, and all of us, including me, also were unable to see the text to be read. In addition, between us and the book was a cardboard shield against the leakage of information. Rosa touched the book from under the shield, read the indicated couple of lines, and only after that did we look at the page. She was perfectly correct, every time! Every word!

Prof. Romanovsky changed the shields. Even one made of iron was not a hindrance and did not alter the results. We changed the distances, too. This did make a difference when Rosa was tired. At a distance of more than one meter the answers began to be less exact, and came more slowly. Rosa also hesitated some seconds before giving the answers in her loud, sharp manner. But I think that the reason for this was primarily psychological. When she was tired or nervous (and she had enough reasons for it—as did all of us), it was generally difficult for her to concentrate and the factor of distance gave her a feeling of uncertainty. Yet, if she was in the mood for it, she could correctly and in detail describe a house hundreds of meters away, which we were to visit later. She also predicted episodes which would occur an hour later or the next day in the apartment of our friends where we organized her performances.

I have trained this faculty in my students and do it myself, as well. We can see and hear (clairvoyantly and clairaudiently) objects and events at any distance or at any time. Some of the former students of our experimental and training group on intuitive fore-casting and remote diagnosis could do it as well as myself. Know-ing this, Rosa began to develop these broader abilities. At this point, she was much less exact in this line (new for her) than in her old (dermo-optic) abilities. In her dermo-optic perception Rosa's answers generally came immediately or, with a difficult task, in less than ten to twenty seconds.

The new capacities in Rosa's work were as follows:

1. She could tell what three figure numbers were drawn in the air behind her back, or in her absence. Returning from another room, she put her palm on the exact place in the air, where the finger of the experimenter had moved to write the figures in the air. She made no mistakes and the answers came in five to ten seconds. Perhaps there are some vibrations in the air, or warmth, resulting from the bio-irradiations of the writing finger, which Rosa could feel with her supersensitive skin—which she had trained for twenty (!) years.

2. Several of us would touch a finger to an object (a book, a table, etc.) behind Rosa, who stood with her head covered and eyes bandaged in the corner or in another room, observed by one of us. Her hands had to be covered too, to prevent them from "spying!" —her own expression. (As everyone knows, they can "see!") After some ten to fifteen seconds of moving her fingers and touching the same object, Rosa could say which of us had put a finger on it and even which finger of which hand! She did this without vacillations or mistakes, every evening! It is obvious that this achievement could assist criminologists as well as many other purposes. (But now it is too late because of Rosa's unfortunate death in 1978.)

Rosa's diagnosis by touch was developing, too. But she did not admit that she was a clairvoyant. It seems that she was afraid to be called so (and not without reasons—a person who is claimed to be clairvoyant can be put in a psychiatric hospital and experience many other troubles). She called her gift "sensitiveness" and in-sisted that the only way for her to gather information was through her fingertips, toes, elbows (that is, all extremities), and to a lesser degree through any place on her skin. She could describe a picture or read words, even sitting on them, wholly clothed. But the term "skin vision" she did not like, since she said that it was a sensation rather than seeing. She began to tell us that in recent months she had seen visions behind her closed eyes, in very bright colors, moving as if in a movie. This is all typical for the beginning of real clairvoyance. Many of us who work in this field have experienced the same effects and also observed it during our group-training work at the Bioinformation Laboratory from 1973–75.

Rosa was a very good teacher of these faculties, and she taught methodically, with calm and patience. She helped people to begin by distinguishing between red and blue colors on sheets of paper, and later between their shades, materials and shapes, as the fingers were held ten to fifteen centimeters above the different objects. After first correctly answering under which hand was the red paper and under which the blue one (this question is answered by everyone), she changed the places, the objects, etc. When her students said that they could distinguish the colors only on paper sheets, she secretly placed other objects under their hands to break through the psychological blocks. Virtually any participant in our sessions whom Rosa began to teach, under her guidance developed into a "mini-Rosa!" I saw her put a red apple and a blue bowl under the palm of a blindfolded journalist who did not believe her claims.

She said soothingly: "Be calm. You'll manage it. I have changed the sheets. Or not? Tell us, under which hand is the red one now?" And after a few seconds of hesitation the man correctly identified it. We then showed him that he had distinguished the colors not only on paper, but with objects as well. After this experiment, he was very proud and full of confidence in his own color feeling. All of this was done without any preparation or preliminary exercises and training.

Note to the Updated Version

The first version of this article was written six months prior to the tragic death of Rosa—one of the most important sensitives of the world.* Now we have lost her, shortly after the beginning of official recognition of her abilities and acceptance as a psychic. We hoped that real scientific and scholarly work could begin, and that the wonderful gifts of Rosa (and others) could be known in the right light, described openly and honestly, without continuing the hindrance and difficult years of struggle. Rosa wanted to be useful,

---

* Some researchers believe that Rosa Kuleshova's demonstrations should be considered as cases of mixed mediumship, i.e., that Rosa, like some other well known sensitives, could cheat from time to time, along with demonstrating genuine phenomena. They emphasize the fact that Rosa actually joined the circus for some time where she studied and performed magic. We do not necessarily agree with this interpretation, however, especially since one of us (L.V.) worked with Rosa several times and observed her performance, which seemed to be quite genuine (including correct identification of color sheets placed under several layers of opaque paper, without both Rosa and the experimenters being aware of the colors prior to obtaining Rosa's answers). —Eds.

wanted to teach the blind and to help physicians in making precise diagnoses. There was too much caution, too many obstacles and apprehensions: "it is unknown;" "it is unproven;" "it isn't approved." In any event, it is too late to talk about this now—Rosa is dead. There is no other psychic in the world with such a degree of development of this ability. We hope that this example will help many people to understand and be more careful with talented psychics, to offend them less with aggressive mistrust, to spare their efforts—and even their lives.

Tests in Clairvoyance

Barbara Ivanova

Here Barbara introduces her practices of quasi-visual and quasi-auditory forms of inner seeing and hearing. Following concentration and relaxation, Barbara and her students are able to correctly "see" and "hear" what is happening at distant locations.

In her work with technical diagnosis to determine causes and avoid factory accidents and other technological problems, Barbara concludes that psychic examinations are best established on the information provided by several psychics, rather than one alone. Such applied parapsychological studies are currently being conducted in this country by Bill Kautz and his Research Center for Applied Intuition (61 Renato Ct. #8, Redwood City, CA 94061), Stephen Schwartz of the Mobius Group (2525 Hyperion Ave., Los Angeles, CA 90027), and Russell Targ and Keith Harary of Delphi Associates (66 Bovet Rd., San Mateo, CA 94402).

Naturally, our readers will not be surprised to find Barbara's closing appeal that humankind's psi faculties be used to serve all the people of our planet.—Eds.

■ In training other types of clairvoyance ("receiving intuitive information," as it was called in the author's experimental groups), such as the description of distant places, we proceed with similar techniques to those used by the well known physicists Hal Puthoff and Russell Targ (although we have no means for such a good organization of the experiments as they have!). In the foretelling of various facts and events (which the author terms "intuitive forecasting," and the forms of it "quasi-visual" and "quasi-auditory expressions"), we use specific forms of psycho-mobilization before we begin our experiments, for example, some types of conscious autoregulation. In individual tests of good psychics, however, we need no preparations, other than our usual concentration and relaxation techniques for one to three minutes, which facilitate the information flow for the optimization of the inner conditions of the psychic in the realization of his task. I would like to briefly mention two experiments (from many hundreds of them), and quote excerpts from our records.

1. The first was conducted in one of the Moscow research laboratories in the summer of 1977 (I will not give the name of the laboratory as well as the names of the participants due to obvious reasons*). The subject (myself) was together with a group of researchers (which included a Doctor of Physics and Mathematics, an M.D., and several Ph.D.s and engineers) in one of the rooms of the laboratory. My task was to describe another room which was behind two walls, that is, the third room from this one. The distance to the walls of the second and third rooms was ten and thirteen meters. I had to describe all the things which were located between these walls and not to confuse them with what was behind the first wall in the adjacent room.

The experimenter explained to the other participants that I was here for the first time and had never before been in the other rooms of the laboratory. Three individuals knew some of the contents in the target room, but not in all the details, and their presence could influence telepathically only a part of the data.

After two minutes of relaxation and concentration (expectance stimulation) I began to tell the impressions which appeared in my inner vision—the quasi-visual sensations, as I term them. I described the objects (a part of which were hidden under some covers and unknown to anyone) and their shapes and colors in minute detail. I incorrectly placed into the target room one object from the adjacent room.

In general we could say that the results were ninety percent positive. There are very few psychics who can give one hundred percent positive results. Even Rosa Kuleshova was not always absolutely correct. It depends on many factors, primarily the well known experimenter effect, since there must be a positive, friendly atmosphere during the tests.

2. Another case was more significant: I was asked to intuitively find reasons for an accident which had happened due to an equipment failure a year prior to this experiment. At the time of the test, a commission of engineers did not have a unanimous opinion about the reasons for the accident. I was not told either the external

---

* In the Soviet Union, any paper intended for publication abroad has to be officially evaluated and approved. This evaluation is possible only if the author works at an official research institution. If this is not the case, and if the author dares to publish a paper abroad without this approval, he/she usually tries to eliminate references to other participants in order not to have them responsible for an unauthorized publication and thus, to spare them much trouble.—Eds.

appearance nor the purpose of the equipment. Since I am an educator and language instructor by profession, my knowledge in the field of technology is very limited, and I had to get information only in an intuitive (clairvoyant) way. This test was conducted by technical diagnosis, a new line of research for me. I have organized this training, investigated it, and presently am preparing a series of articles about it based on our experiments. In technical diagnosis I try to ascertain various defects of an apparatus, hidden from view and remote in space and time. Using intuitive diagnosis I try to learn the causes of accidents, damages in the past, and possible dangers in the future. I started this work in 1974 and try to pursue it as best as I can.

The dialogue between the experimenter (a member of the commission of engineers) and the psi-diagnostician-operator (myself) went as follows:

Experimenter: "How many defects were there in the equipment?"

Operator: "It seems to me, three. Yes, I see the number 3."

Experimenter: "What were the defects?"

Operator: "I see a convex component, in the form of a hemisphere of bright-yellow color. It did not fit closely, and there was a clearance."

Experimenter: "There was such a component, so this was possible. What else was there?"

Operator: "I see a long, flat, dark detail. There were many grooves on it. I feel that it jammed."

Experimenter: "Correct. This was a restrictor. Such a defect was also possible. What else can you tell?"

Operator: "I see a glittering piece. It seems to be nickel-plated. Its size is as follows (she showed the size with her hands). It had a small crack inside. In the course of the equipment's functioning it gradually enlarged. The piece did not stand the load and broke."

Experimenter: "It is quite possible and logical. There is one more important question: could these defects remain unnoticed during tests of the equipment?"

Operator: "I feel that the tests were too short. They had to be as long as the first period of functioning of the equipment. It seems to me that the defects manifested themselves in the second half of the period of the equipment's functioning."

Experimenter: "Well, it is quite possible. Please describe the people who operated the equipment, and their positions during the accident."

A description followed which, according to the experimenter, was quite correct, including descriptions of the faces, clothes, postures and surroundings of the workers. I believe, however, that in serious cases such examinations should not be based on the information of one sensitive. It is necessary to invite several sensitives, and to work independently with each of them. A statistical processing of the obtained intuitive information should follow. It is also clear that, for a scientifically valid controlled experiment, the person(s) familiar with the equipment/situation under discussion should not be in the same room with the sensitive, or conduct the interview.

Conclusion

I did not present many details here and did not mention many other experimental cases. The main conclusion is obvious: the faculties called skin vision, intuitive forecasting, receiving intuitive information, etc., have a vast range of application in many important areas. We believe that, despite present difficulties, the situation in the field of parapsychology will change. Not only practical possibilities, but the real, inner meaning and purpose of psi research will become clear and will find its way to serve all the people of our planet.

Intuitive Diagnosis on a Large Scale: From the Human Body to Machines

Barbara Ivanova

In the following selection, Barbara elaborates on her experiments in using intuition to diagnose a situation, including bodily disorders, technical diagnosis (as described previously) and personal occurrences.

Again, Barbara offers her hope and plea that such abilities as those she trains in her students will be accompanied by a moral and humane education. Finally, she urges international guidelines and treaties to prevent the misuse of parapsychological faculties. — Eds.

■ Part of our work involves the education and training of subjects in the use of their natural clairvoyant and telepathic faculties for receiving intuitive information concerning disorders in living systems (medical diagnosis), malfunctions of technical equipment (technical diagnosis), and events separated in space and time from the observer (remote diagnosis of the situation). To a certain extent, some of our attempts are similar to the remote viewing experiments conducted by the reputed American scientists, Targ and Puthoff.[1] Our work began in 1973.[2]

For experimentation we trained in different forms of receiving psi information: quasi-visual perception (clairvoyance); quasi-auditory (clairaudience) and other quasi-feelings (such as physical sensations); "information-PK";[3] etc. Before beginning the experiments, the subjects received specific information about the phenomena (for approximately twenty minutes) and preparatory exercises (fifteen to twenty minutes). Induction procedures included a combination of relaxation techniques, suggestions for mental alertness, and for achieving near-meditation states. The target (disorder, malfunction, or event) to be perceived might have happened in the past, was happening in the present, or was expected to happen in the future. The target could be at a distance of a few feet or thousands of miles from the subject. Some examples along the three lines of our studies are given below.

I. **Diagnosis of bodily disorders**. These tests were conducted in the author's experimental and training group for intuitive fore-casting and distance-image diagnosis:[2,5]

Test 1: Thirty participants. Target: a scar on the head, not visible, under the hair, in the form of a sickle. Five subjects localized it, one gave the exact dimension and form. Twenty individuals gave approximate answers.

Test 2: Thirty participants. Target: a scar on the left foot of a person. (It is important to stress that the target-person did not remember, at least consciously, on which of his feet it was, and so the telepathic way of information-escape was minimal.) Two persons gave the exact shape and localization while the others received aspects of the right answer.

Test 3: Twenty-three participants. Target A: rupture (hernia). Two subjects obtained the right answer, and fifteen others received approximate ones. Target B: two toes of the target-person's right foot were amputated. Three participants reported that they were perceiving a dark spot on this place. As always, sixty to seventy percent of the audience got different, approximate, but related answers. Target C: scars in the form of crosses on both palms, soles, and on one knee. Twenty participants reported that they "saw" dark spots or even felt pain on these places of their own body (quasi-feelings). The target person sat with his palms down and it was impossible to guess the unusual forms at so many places on the body.

Test 4: Thirty-five participants. Target pain in the heart and liver. Forty percent of the audience drew the places correctly, while also feeling pains on their bodies in these places.

The number of correspondences corroborating the impressions of the subjects and the targets in general is seventy to eighty percent, but vary in type and are therefore difficult for more detailed quantitative evaluation.

II. **Technical Diagnosis.** One of the experiments of such a kind has already been described in the articles entitled "Psi in Action" and "Tests in Clairvoyance."[6,7] In the test, I (as operator-diagnostician) had to find out the causes of an accident which had happened a year prior to the experiment. According to the commission of scientists, the description of equipment (which I had never seen) and causes of the accident which I identified were quite correct. I believe that this type of diagnosis is of particular importance and can be significant in preventing accidents, crashes, and other unfortunate occurrences.

III. **Intuitive diagnosis of the situation.** The following incident, related to the author by a woman from Sukhumi (USSR), represents an example of remote perception.[8] Several years ago, she suddenly heard a voice, "You will never see your son." The voice was so clear that she even asked out loud, "Why?" But no one was there and she was alone. The next day she received a telegram informing her that her son had drowned at the same moment she had heard the voice. Her daughter had a dream the same night: "My heart was cut in half. I felt terrible pain! And I had a feeling that my brother would not come home anymore." A third sign was that the day before the unfortunate occurrence, their dog began digging in the ground near their house. The animal dug for a considerable time and made a deep hole, then howled and ran away. The dog was never seen again.

Many believe that the numerous cases like this are pure coincidence. However, there are too many similar observations to consider them all coincidences. Perhaps further studies of such cases (especially premonitions in animals) will enable researchers to better understand psi phenomena.

Conclusions

Clairvoyance (both spatial and temporal) may be trained and applied practically in medical diagnosis, technology, criminology, science, arts, etc., as a supplement to other, more accepted ways. But the main point, which is often understated in works about parapsychology, concerns the moral, ethical, and educational aspects. If we train our subjects only practically, without any human education, or any explanation about their responsibility for what they do, there are negative consequences. We cannot consider science without an ethical basis, least of all so powerful a discipline as parapsychology. Like any teacher, educator, or instructor, we must educate in our students not only technical skills, but human qualities. If we do not develop their *sense of justice, integrity, fairness,* etc., they may use their talents (or permit others to use them) for negative, dangerous goals. We have the duty to help them to distinguish and avoid such a catastrophe. We must also create objective preconditions for averting the global danger of any antihuman use of parapsychological faculties, and organize against it through the *development of comprehensive international guidelines*.

References

1. Puthoff, H.E., & Targ, R. "A Perceptual Channel for Information Transfer over Kilometer Distances: Historical Perspective and Recent Research," *Proceedings of the IEEE*, Vol. 64, March 1976, pp. 329–354.

2. Ivanova, B. "Comment apprendre à se souvenir du futur: Methode d'entrainement à la précognition," *Psi Réalités* (Paris), No. 10, 1978, pp. 24–27 (in French).

3. Ivanova, B. "Information-Bearing PK (Psychokinesis)," *New Frontiers Center Newsletter* (Oregon, Wis.), No. 1, January–March 1982, pp. 2–3.

4. Ivanova, B. "Theoretical Concepts of Distant Healing and Clairvoyant Diagnostics," *Psychic Observer* (Washington, D.C.), Vol. 39, No. 3, 1981, pp. 225–231.

5. Ivanova, B. "Some Training Experiments in Clairvoyance," *Proceedings of the Fifth International Conference on Psychotronic Research*, Vol. 3, Bratislava, 1983, pp. 162–167.

6. "Psi in Action," *Psi Research* (San Francisco, Ca.), Vol. 1, No. 1, March 1982, pp. 39–40.

7. Ivanova, B. "Tests in Clairvoyance," present collection, pp. 72-75.

8. Ivanova, B. "You Will Never See Your Son...," *Psi Research* (San Francisco, Ca.), Vol. 1, No. 2, June 1982, p. 102.

Some Aspects of Information-PK Experiments; Information-Bearing Psychokinesis

Barbara Ivanova

In the following selection, Barbara emerges as a teacher, accompanied by her thoughtful approach to psi phenomena. For both students and researchers of psi, she offers concrete and practical suggestions. To assist in receiving psi information, Barbara's open-minded attitude is revealed as she discusses the process of a dowser asking advice of the "source." How one individually defines the source is a personal and unique decision, she notes; what she advises is to ask clear and specific questions.

As always, Barbara urges spiritual and moral development along-side psi development.—Eds.

■ According to our observations and experiments, some PK (psychokinetic) phenomena can be regarded as "detector-indicators" of psi information about important circumstances and facts.[1] According to Dr. C.T.K. Chari (Madras, India), there are four types of information that are of importance to biological systems:[2]

First, there is the genetic information which determines inherited characteristics and instructs the functioning of cells and is passed on from one generation to the next. Second, there is environmental information. This is largely Man's sensory input from nature: his reactions to temperature and humidity, to light and dark—all fed directly into the nervous system. Unlike genetic information, the environmental kind is not passed on from generation to generation. Third, Chari considers information at the distinctly human level: the communication of verse and prose, spoken language and written symbols. And fourth, Chari suggests the existence of a "psi-information system": a full system in its own right, but operating on different principles than the other three. For that difference, Chari turns to quantum theory.[2]

We can divide the information-PK phenomena roughly into two sub-groups:

I. **Telekinesis:** *Actions at a distance without a visible or detectable contact.* These can occur at distances of thousands of miles. Such forms of telekinesis-actions might include:

1. Some poltergeist phenomena, such as the so-called "death-coincidences," raps, or knocks.[3]
2. Psychic photography (thoughtography) of different types (appearance of paranormal images on photographic film).[4]
3. Dermography or dermographism (appearance of marks on human skin, voluntarily or involuntarily, including stigmata).[5]
4. "Direct" writing, painting, designing, etc. (paranormal production of written messages, drawings, or pictures which appear without any visible causes or with a pen writing by itself).[6]
5. Levitation of objects when occurring in response to a question.
6. Some occurrences thought to be "good" or "bad" omens.
7. Voices of unknown origin recorded on magnetic tapes.[7]
8. Some divination practices where there is a change of position of the objects used.
9. Some cases of distant and "super" distant healing, with physical results such as dissolution of calcium, elimination of tumors and other detectable changes in the physiological state and structure of the body. The influence of the healer and the response of the body could perhaps be regarded as information-PK.

II. **Parakinesis:** *Actions on inert matter which require some point of contact—a certain contact which nevertheless seems inadequate to cause the information-movement of the tools used.* These include dowsing (using a dowsing rod, pendulum, and similar devices), use of planchettes, and psychography ("automatic" writing and painting). The information received in these ways may be scientific ideas, art, solutions to general life problems, finding minerals, underwater and underground ancient constructions, missing persons and objects, personal advice, medical consultation, solution of criminal cases, different events which have occurred in other places and times, and many other kinds of information.

It is known that some gifted people can get exteriorizations of quasi-visual images and projections on such different "screens" as crystals, lenses, water-glasses, walls, etc. They can also unconsciously express their inner (psychically received) knowledge in PK forms, that is, in the symbolic movement of different objects.

The tools and instruments like a dowsing rod or pendulum are necessary and work only when the subject cannot get the psi information *inwardly* and *needs* the *outward* expression through different tools. We have observed that after a time, with the development of psi faculties, the individual begins to receive the needed answers directly in his/her mind, and the mechanical forms of receiving psi information are no longer needed.

It is important to emphasize that if one has a high degree of psi abilities—and a great percentage of people have them without knowing it—one must use them, not suppress them. The results of suppression of psi-faculties are complexes, fears, stress, incommunicability, and even worse problems. Many medical and social problems arise as a result of "psi-negativism," ignorance, or incorrect interpretation of psi phenomena.

If psi experiments involve answers to questions, as in pendulum practice and some other divination practices, we must observe certain *moral* and *ethical* rules as to the content of the question. We have had much evidence in our work which has shown that if we neglect this principal rule of psycho-hygiene, the results may be disastrous. Be careful! Also, we must attain a certain level of knowledge and spiritual development before we can get accurate information. Do not rely too much on messages in the beginning of your practice. Here is some advice as to what we need to get the right answers:

1. Do not anticipate the responses, but remain detached from them.
2. Do not let the mind wander off the question or you may get indications of whatever you are thinking about.
3. Do not fight the movements of the indicator—the pendulum, dowsing rod, etc., that you may be using.
4. Mind and body must be relaxed for maximum success.
5. When you are seeking personal gain, guilt and self-

centeredness may tend to block the path of information from the source and result in incorrect information.

6. At the very least, pain or other physical problems act as distractions and may somehow block the response.
7. Stay at least ten to fifteen feet away from skeptical on-lookers and request them to remain silent.
8. The movements of the instruments can be programmed consciously to give meaning to the unconscious response.
9. Clear and specific questioning of the "source" (irrespective of what you imply by this notion) is important for receiving clear answers.

All these recommendations can be used not only in dowsing practices, but are suitable for other forms of psi as well. We have enumerated these means for psi information, along with advice on how to use them, in the hope that we can help researchers and psychics on their way to knowledge of psi.

References

1. Ivanova, B. "Information-Bearing PK (Psychokinesis)," *New Frontiers Center Newsletter* (Oregon, Wis.), No. 1, January–March 1982.
2. Panati, C. "Quantum Physics and Parapsychology: Twenty-third International Conference of the Parapsychology Foundation," *Parapsychology Review*, Vol. 5, No. 6, November–December 1974, pp. 1–5.
3. Playfair, G.L. *The Flying Cow: Research into Paranormal Phenomena in the World's Most Psychic Country*, London: Souvenir Press, 1975.
4. Eisenbud, J. *The World of Ted Serios*, New York: Morrow, 1967.
5. Barber, T.X. "Experimental Hypnosis," In B.B. Wolman (Ed.), *Handbook of General Psychology*, Englewood Cliffs, N.J.: Prentice-Hall, 1973, pp. 942–963.
6. "PK and Metal-Bending in Italy: Observations and Experiments (Interviews with Dr. Paola Giovetti and Dr. Ferdinando Bersani," *Psi Research* (San Francisco, Ca.), Vol. 1, No.3, 1982, pp. 22–26.
7. Raudive, K. *Breakthrough*, New York: Lancer Books, 1971.

Terminological or Substantial Differences?

Larissa Vilenskaya

■ In the 1930s, when scientific studies of psi phenomena were nascent, researchers preferred to speak separately about telepathy, clairvoyance, and precognition. However, it soon became clear that it is extremely difficult to make a clear delineation: if the sender (inductor) looks at a drawing and the subject (receiver) in an adjacent room or at a distance of 1,000 miles makes the same drawing, we have in fact three possibilities: (a) the subject received the information of the image from the brain of the sender; (b) the subject received information directly from the drawing; (c) the subject "traveled" in time forward to the moment of verification of the result of the test (when he was actually shown the drawing), picked up the information "then" and "brought" it into the past. Different experimental designs were used to enable researchers to isolate only one phenomenon and exclude other options, but the realization of the complexity of this problem leads to the situation which exists today: researchers prefer to speak of ESP in general and combine telepathy, clairvoyance, and precognition, and not to mention each phenomenon separately.

The delineation between ESP and PK phenomena is also not so simple. I will further explain my point by citing a precognitive case from an excellent collection of spontaneous psi cases by Louisa E. Rhine:[1]

> In Washington state a young woman was so upset by a terrifying dream one night that she had to wake her husband and tell him about it. She had dreamed that a large ornamental chandelier which hung over their baby's bed in the next room had fallen into the crib and crushed the baby to death. In the dream she could see herself and her husband standing amid the wreckage. The clock on the baby's dresser said 4:35. In the distance she could hear the

rain on the windowpane and wind blowing outside. But her husband just laughed at her. He said it was a silly dream, to forget it and go back to sleep; and in matter of moments he did just that himself. But she could not sleep. Finally, still frightened, she got out of bed and went to the baby's room, got her and brought her back. On the way she stopped to look out the window, and saw a full moon, the weather calm and quite unlike the dream. Then, though feeling a little foolish, she got back into bed with the baby. About two hours later they were wakened by a resounding crash. She jumped up, followed by her husband, and ran to the nursery. There, where the baby would have been lying, was the chandelier in the crib. They looked at each other and then at the clock. It stood at 4:35. Still a little skeptical they listened—to the sound of rain on the windowpane and wind howling outside.

Thus, evidently this is a case of pure premonition: the foreseen event happened but fortunately no one was injured or killed due to the precognitive dream. However, one can think of another possibility: the woman was so frightened by the dream (the reason for which might not be psi information, but a mother's concern for her baby), that, after taking the baby from the nursery and feeling that she was safe, she unconsciously used her psychokinetic powers to influence the chandelier, making it fall down at the exact time of her dream. Although moments of her dream about weather speak against this possibility, from what we know about manifestations of psi it cannot be completely ruled out, at least theoretically. This question (ESP or PK) becomes even more complicated in tests with random number generators which have been conducted by numerous researchers throughout the last decade.[2,3] When an individual makes an assessment as to which random number the computer will display next, does he predict this event or does he attempt to influence the computer to choose this exact number? Therefore, many researchers prefer to speak not about ESP and PK, but about psi in general.

Everyone agrees that we do not know much about psi phenomena, their nature and conditions of occurrence. In this situation, is it worthwhile to attempt any classification of these phenomena, to try to find its own "shelf," or a term for each of the strange events and occurrences? On the other hand, systematization has always been an important tool in science—one can remember the discovery (via a dream) of Periodic Law by Dmitry Mendeleyev, which he began by elaborating upon a convenient table to present chemical elements known at that time. Although some elements were unknown and the table had a number of gaps, he managed to detect the periodicity of elements which enabled him to predict new elements (discovered later) and to bring chemistry to a qualitatively new level. The same can be true for psi research. Therefore, despite the difficulties involved, I believe Barbara's attempt to distinguish information-PK phenomena is extremely important.

I first learned of a case of information-PK from a friend of mine, Luda M., more than fifteen years ago. We finished high school together in the Ukrainian town of Poltava, and I later went to study in Moscow. Returning to Poltava for a visit, I always was very happy to see her. Once, coming to Poltava, I found her very distressed: her father had died a few months before. His death was unexpected—he fainted at work, was taken to the hospital and died from a brain hemorrhage without regaining consciousness. This happened so quickly that when Luda and her mother were informed at their jobs and came immediately to the hospital, he was already dead. When they returned home, they found that a large thermos was broken and broken glass with a shining silver surface was scattered all over the room. There were no pets in the apartment to do this, and, while cleaning the room of broken glass, Luda could find no other reason except that this was a sign of the death of her father. This case seems to me quite convincing.

At the same time, I am skeptical as to the necessity of distinguishing the category of parakinesis which would include dowsing and related phenomena. The common viewpoint is that a dowsing rod or pendulum are turned into motion by slight unconscious (ideomotor) muscle movements of the dowser in response to subliminal (subsensory) or psi information. Therefore, although these "instruments" can be detectors of psi information, we do not have sufficient evidence to consider this process as "mind over matter" influence. It is also true that experienced dowsers often do not need the instruments and prefer so-called deviceless dowsing.

One of the most interesting descriptions of this technique I found in the paper "From Devices to Deviceless Dowsing," delivered by Jaddie Stoddard at the Twenty-Second Convention of the American Society of Dowsers in Danville, Vermont, in September

1982. While listening to her talk, I remembered the poetic lines from the fairy tales of my childhood:

> Mirror, mirror on the wall,
> Who's the fairest of them all?

One might object that despite these lines (as poetic as they are), clairvoyants of all times and nations have preferred to ask not the mirror, but rather a crystal ball. And while gazing at the crystal, many of them seemed to receive the answers to their questions. However, Jaddie Stoddard, who described her uncommon technique at the Dowsing Convention, to my great amazement addressed questions to visualized traffic lights instead of a crystal ball!

Jaddie Stoddard inherited dowsing abilities from her father. Despite her father's warning about using dowsing for anything but water and metal, which he claimed could result in losing one's abilities, she successfully applies dowsing to a great variety of tasks.

"Using your pendulum or any other similar 'device,' you can do anything and ask anything," this slim, lively woman—who once worked as an investigative reporter—told the convention participants. "But I believe that for some people all these devices are unnecessary. You can simply ask your question and get an answer. The first step is to clearly define what your 'yes' and what your 'no' is."

Indeed, everyone who has had some experience with dowsing knows that "yes" may be indicated by a dowsing rod moving sideways or up and down in your hands, or a pendulum moving in a clockwise or counterclockwise direction, etc. Jaddie Stoddard, in working out a method which she later called deviceless dowsing, imagined that she "saw" traffic lights on her mental screen, while asking her question. Quite simply, green meant "yes" to her, red —"no," yellow—"reformulate the question."

"Take this technique home and try it," she suggested. "If this does not work, maybe you need to come up with something else. Listen to your intuition. Dowsing is not a 100% certainty, and you have to be prepared for this. But everyone can try and be successful."

Explaining her approach, Stoddard listed the following rules which, in her opinion, a dowser should observe in order to be successful:

1. Assume nothing.
2. Learn to relax the body and keep the mind alert.
3. Ask the "right" questions.
4. Practice, practice, and practice.
5. Be prepared to be discouraged and less than perfect.
6. Keep detailed records: questions, answers, verifications.
7. Enjoy learning about yourself, about others and about the Universe.
8. Learn what is right for you.
9. Assume total responsibility for your actions.
10. Discipline the mind; learn to recognize certain signals.
11. Don't strain for answers, don't push—it won't work.
12. Learn to grow without setting limits on yourself.

One can easily see that these rules perfectly supplement Barbara's recommendations. I believe that, irrespective of our attitude to these rules and recommendations from a scientific point of view, it is helpful to have some guidelines which have already worked for someone else.

References

1. Rhine, L.E. *Hidden Channels of the Mind*, New York: Sloane, 1961, pp. 198-199.
2. Schmidt, H. "Psychokinesis," In E.D. Mitchell & J. White (Eds.), *Psychic Exploration: A Challenge for Science*, New York: Putnam's, 1974, pp. 179–193.
3. Jahn, R.G. "The Persistent Paradox of Psychic Phenomena: An Engineering Perspective," *Proceedings of the IEEE*, Vol. 70, No. 2, February 1982, pp. 136–170.

Psychography and Parapictography as Ways of Receiving Intuitive Information

Barbara Ivanova

Here Barbara discusses the phenomenon of "psi-painting" in which an individual, while in altered state of consciousness, automatically produces high quality works of art.

We have worked extensively with the Brazilian psi artist, Luis Gasparetto, of São Paulo. Watching Luis work is a most remarkable opportunity. He stands over six feet tall, handsome, fair skinned, eyes of oceanic depth, and possessed of that sweet-strong and irresistible Brazilian charm.

Luis sits at a long table, before large sheets of paper, a pile of crayon-chalks, and boxes of multi-colored paint tubes. There is a small lamp with a red bulb nearby. When the lights are turned out in the room, the red lamp, illuminating only the forms, washes color out of the chalks and paints and people. The *Four Seasons* begins to play quite loudly, as Luis closes his eyes and sways to Vivaldi's symphony. In a few moments, Luis reaches quickly toward the chalks, picks up one, and begins to draw hurriedly. Chalks begin to roll and fly as he moves faster and faster, scribbling quickly with several colors, then sliding the paper aside and beginning another. In the strange red light and with the speed of Luis' hands—since he uses both simultaneously—colors and forms are impossible to discern. Attention is drawn to Luis, his eyes closed and head cocked to one side, moving perfectly to Vivaldi as his hands scratch and fly across the paper.

He works this way for fully one to one and one-half hours. At some point in the time, he will switch to the paints—quick drying acrylics. Eyes closed, he twists open the tubes and begins squeezing them into his left palm, using it as the palette for his right hand. After sixty to ninety minutes, he stops, and usually excuses himself to clean his hands.

The lights are turned on once again, and the twenty to twenty-five finished paintings are displayed. They are extraordinary works of art—representing the styles of some forty different masters—Monet, Picasso, Toulouse-Lautrec, Renoir, Gauguin. Most of the paintings are portraits, and the presentation of each artist is unique and unmistakable. The strokes are dynamic and sure, the painting is alive and vibrant, the use of color and shading is articulate and lovely.

After viewing the paintings, the audience is invited to stay and talk informally with Luis. He explains his belief that in his altered state of consciousness, which is impelled by concentration on the music, he is able to receive intuitive information from the "invisible energy" fields which contain the personalities we know on earth as the great masters. His paintings are convincing.

When asked why he publicly demonstrates his skill to people, free of charge, he replies, "To show people that our existence *does* con-

tinue after death, and for this reason, we must live with care and love for ourselves, for all beings, and for our Earth."

In this selection, Barbara looks into both the positive and negative aspects of psi development: talented young Vasya, a psychic artist, and an elderly woman lacking sufficient moral and spiritual development to pursue her psi abilities.—Eds.

■ The term psychography is broadly used in Russia to denote automatic writing, drawing, etc. Formerly the expression "psi-painting" was used to describe automatic artistic production, yet for this branch of psychography we now employ the term "parapicto-graphy," adopted mainly from Brazilian researchers. We have conducted studies in this field, and have interpreted the cases we have encountered in its various branches.

Depending on the state of the subject's mind we distinguish two types of phenomena: (a) Complete awareness of the process without knowing the source of information, and a personal non-involvement in it. (b) Total unawareness of the process, with no control of the conscious self or participation of judgment and analysis during the information-process. We do not believe that the expression "automatic" fully describes the process, since complete passivity can be spontaneous or can be induced by trance, semi-trance, or meditation. The two types mentioned above are not mutually exclusive, they can sometimes occur in combination. In actual cases we observe the phenomena changing from one type into another either during a session or between sessions. According to our analysis, the first type usually pertains to a well-educated intellectual person, and the second type to persons without education.

If an individual is a gifted psychic subject, psi capabilities often manifest themselves in multiple form. In the course of my research, I have explored some hypotheses and theoretical considerations of these cases. Here I would like only to make some general remarks and describe some cases of interest. The phenomena relating to psychography can be divided, according to the means of expression, into three main types: (a) *in words*: all types of writings (fiction, poetry, scientific work); (b) *in images*: painting, drawing (parapictography), visual art or science; (c) *in symbols*: fiction, art, and science. Here we can also refer mathematical formulae, musical notes, abstract forms of art, etc. These three types of expression often mix or merge together.

One of the mixed cases was that of Vasya M., whom I met in the Caucausus in the summer of 1976. Vasya is primarily gifted in psi-art. Although he has never studied the arts, he is a talented painter and carver, and his paintings are awarded grants and prizes. Vasya creates his works of art very quickly, and they are of various styles and manners, almost as if many painters were dwelling inside him. According to experts, some of his pictures resemble the techniques of old masters, yet he appears to know nothing about them. He learns the various styles in an altered state resembling somnolence or drowsiness. He once told me that under such a state his hands move independently of his will. He had never heard of psychography before I informed him of it.

Vasya becomes oblivious to his environment and sees it "from afar," while his hands draw sketches for the future picture which he has not yet conceived. Then his hand makes circular movements on the canvas or paper without any effort of will or intention. Vasya feels as if it is not he who is painting, and is often surprised when he sees what he has painted. The same is true of the psychographers and parapictographers whom I have met or read about.

Most impressive is Vasya's almost life-size painting of a weary old man sitting with his shoulders bent and sadly contemplating his rusty plough. The picture is very simple, but it has a strange effect on viewers who study it: their hearts miss a beat, their breath stops. Vasya told me about the creation of this picture: "I suddenly felt the urge to paint. It is always so for me. I feel I have to paint, yet I do not know exactly what or how; I never plan. I sat quietly at the table, and my pencil moved, drawing some apparently random lines on the paper. Falling half asleep, I could not perceive what would emerge at the end. As always, I looked at my hand moving quickly with the pencil clenched in it, making chaotic lines on the paper. Suddenly I saw a tired old man, sitting in a sad posture, with a tragic expression on his face. I actually felt how his shoulders, so strong and broad before, were stooping under the burden of life. I felt his troubles as if they were my own. I saw him as he was many years before, young and strong, plowing the soil. But the war broke out and he had to abandon his home. Years flew by. He returned to find his house destroyed, and only the plough was left, rusty and broken. Now he is wondering what to do.

"The picture was soon complete. By the way, I usually apply the final touches in a state of complete consciousness. A few days later a young woman, my neighbor, happened to glance at the picture: 'How fine it looks, very life-like—I know him well. When he came home after the war he found his house burned down. So you know him too? You can read the whole story on his face, here on the canvas.'

"Naturally I had no notion of whom she was talking about, though the details were familiar to me. It came in a flash. How could it happen that I penetrated so deeply into the life and fate of a stranger? And it happens often. What is this force I have? How does it descend on me?"

In a national competition in 1976 Vasya was awarded a prize for the high artistic quality of his stage set for a production of the opera *Don Carlos*. Now he is a famous set designer though he has never studied the art. His theater sets are characterized by a conciseness of expression, dynamism and austerity which are not really characteristic of him as a person. He also paints and makes wood-carvings of various kinds. Sometimes his face vaguely expresses the stamp of another personality, and I believe it probably was he in a former incarnation.

Here is an interesting case of a different type. An elderly lady was very much interested in psychography and began to practice it under my instruction. However, she did not sufficiently possess the necessary moral and ethical values without which no real psi abilities should be developed. (It is often difficult to evaluate the stage which a person has really achieved. When one is not sufficiently ready, the practice can bring negative results and even harm the person. So all psychics and experimenters must be careful!)

A circle of friends gathered at my home to practice psychography. Since no psi training should last more than fifteen to twenty minutes lest the psychics mind and body suffer ill-effects, we took a break to rest. The woman continued to practice alone, disregarding the rules. We were occupied with our own noisy, carefree conversation and paid no attention to her occasional shrieks, believing them not to be serious. Then she shouted louder. Becoming alarmed, we ran up to her and found her lying on the table laughing and crying hysterically, her hand clenching a pencil and drawing wild lines and circles on the tablecloth.

"Help, hold it! Stop it!" she cried. This behavior was quite out of character with this well-bred woman. With great difficulty we restrained her hand and took the pencil out of her clenched fist. I forbade her to train further in psychography before she first purified her mind and body with special preparations, lectures, and diet. After some time she began to train in healing and psychometry, which was less dangerous to her. Attacks similar to the one described above did not recur.

I would like to cite here another case, that of a thirty-five year old woman. I noticed that while talking or thinking of something else, the woman often unconsciously drew the classical signs which resemble a continuous chain of the letter S or number eight. These are known to be evidence of abilities in psychography and an unconscious expression of self-training. I briefly explained to her the nature of her gift, and gave her some training methods and direction. A couple of months later I saw her again. Her friends now jokingly called her a witch since she was able to automatically deliver in writing answers to their questions about the past and the future which later proved true. Before she began her psychographic activities, the woman had been nervous and ill-tempered. She had suffered from headaches, and cramps in her arms and hands. When I saw her again her eyes were full of joy. We know that psychography, as with many other manifestations of psi abilities, when done properly and observing all the psycho-hygienic rules, can be beneficial for a person and even cure him/her of such negative states of mind and body as faints, epilepsy, cramps, or nervous tension.

Can One See the Future?

Barbara Ivanova

Barbara has coined the term "intuitive forecasting" to refer to that phenomenon by which an individual can accurately foretell future events, usually termed precognition. In this selection, Barbara considers the nature, some explanations, and several uses for intuitive forecasting. We conclude with an abstract of a paper by Larissa and Barbara considering methodology for the development of conscious control of intuitively received information. — Eds.

Prophecies of Writers and Scientists

■ Amongst the many examples we could quote, a notable one is the story of Kolbe, the German chemist of the 19th century, who, during an argument, invented what he thought were sixteen totally absurd variations of the structure of the molecule of an organic compound. As it turned out, every one of these variations was discovered several years later!

The foreword to the *Collected Works* (Vol. 1) of the famous Soviet science fiction writer Alexander Kazantsev[1] stated: "Cosmonaut Georgi Beregovoi in his book, *The Angle of the Attack*, wrote: 'Kazantsev long ago foresaw in principle the construction of the contemporary 'moon walker' and made a mistake only in describing the element as a 'caterpillar transmission.' Yet, Kazantsev described a 'moon walker' in his novel *The Moon's Road* in 1959, when scientists had not even dreamed about the landing of a 'moon walker' on the moon's surface.' " Virtually all technical details were identical!

There have been many other similar facts as well as spontaneous observations and laboratory studies of precognition which require scientific explanation.

A Few Questions and Answers About Precognition

1. **What** is precognition? The *Great Soviet Encyclopedia*[2] defines it as: "Foresight (precognition)—a particular instance of clairvoyance, related to forecasting future events." Clairvoyance, in turn, is defined as follows: "Obtaining knowledge of objective events of the external world not based on known senses and reasoning."

2. **Where** do the phenomena occur about which we can obtain precognitive information? They can occur at any place, at any distance, at any spot on the Earth—or perhaps in the entire Universe.

3. **When** do the phenomena occur? They can take place at any time, a minute or many centuries after receiving precognitive information. The difference is purely psychological, and the "effort" is the same (at least, we do not presently have information which would allow us to answer this question differently, although further studies may change this viewpoint).

4. **In which state** of consciousness does it occur? At any time in a normal waking state, but, more often, in an altered state: sleep, trance, hypnosis, etc.

How Can One Explain Precognition?

1. A latent period in an unconscious decision-making process may give the "psychic" a telepathic hint about some future plans and actions of the individual.

2. Unconscious calculation in which the brain, acting like a computer, processes a number of variables (obtained both consciously and unconsciously, by both sensory and extrasensory means) and arrives at a forecast. The process is usually unconscious, and the result comes as an unexpected insight, hunch, premonition, or prophecy.

3. The concept of *noosphere* developed by Teilhard de Chardin and Soviet Academician Vernadsky, as well as Jung's concept of "collective unconscious" make it possible to assume that the abovementioned brain computer may obtain and unconsciously process much more information than is ordinarily believed.

4. Recent ideas and discoveries in physics suggest the possibility of the existence of yet unknown properties of time (as suggested

by Soviet astrophysicist Nikolai Kozyrev) and multidimensional space/time models.

Issues of precognition were discussed in a very interesting paper by two American physicists, Harold Puthoff and Russell Targ.[3] In the chapter "Considerations Concerning Time" they wrote about the phenomenon of precognitive remote viewing which they encountered in their experiments. In their "normal" remote-viewing tests, a subject described a randomly selected remote location simultaneously with the presence of the outbound experimenters at this location. In precognitive tests, the subject attempted to perform not only spatial, but also temporal remote viewing: he/she gave an accurate description of the target *before* it was randomly selected and before the experimenters arrived there.

The authors emphasize that there exists "copious literature describing years of precognition experiments carried out in various laboratories." They state:

"It is well known and recently has been widely discussed that nothing in the fundamental laws of physics forbids the apparent transmission of information from the future to the present...."

"Currently, we have no precise model of this spatial and temporal remote-viewing phenomenon. However, models of the universe involving higher order synchronicity or correlation have been proposed by physicist Pauli and psychologist Carl Jung:[4]

ACAUSALITY. If natural law (as usually understood) were an absolute truth, then of course there could not possibly be any process that deviates from it. But since causality (as usually understood) is a *statistical* truth, it holds good only on the average and thus leaves room for *exceptions* which must somehow be experienced, that is to say, *real*. I try to regard synchronistic events as acausal exceptions of this kind. They prove to be relatively independent of space and time; they relativize space and time insofar as space presents in principle no obstacle to their passage, and the sequence of events in time is inverted so that it looks as if an event which has not yet occurred were causing a perception in the present."[3]

The researchers state further:

"It is important to note at the outset that many contemporary physicists are of the view that the phenomena that we have been discussing are not at all inconsistent with the framework of physics as currently understood. In this emerging view, the often-held belief that observations of this type are incompatible with known laws *in principle* is erroneous, such a concept being based on the naive realism prevalent before the development of modern quantum theory and information theory."[3]

The authors believe that "although the precise nature of the information channel...is not yet understood...it is recognized that communication theory provides powerful techniques...which can be employed to pursue special-purpose application of the remote-sensing channel independent of an understanding of the underlying mechanisms."[4]

Where Is It Useful?

For many centuries, people have been using precognition for the preservation of life and even of the entire human species. While the biological significance of these qualities is lost in the midst of history, one cannot overestimate the importance of precognition today. Everyone possesses these abilities, but in a latent, unconscious form. Yet, many people use precognition in their everyday life, and this helps them to become better physicians, diagnosticians, scientists, managers, public figures, etc. Professor Samuil Gellershtein in his paper delivered at the congress, "Psychological Problems of Man in Cosmos,"[5] emphasized that "exercises in foreseeing" are an essential part of the training of cosmonauts. He stressed that cosmonauts are required to be able to "respond to events which have not occurred as yet." According to Gellershtein, for training purposes tests have been conducted "to foretell future events, to foresee the nature of future changes in a situation, and to foresee several possible changes which would stimulate alertness for making an optimal decision in the future." In his opinion, the development of these abilities is of particular importance for decision-making in emergency situations.

How Does Humankind Relate to Such Phenomena?

When I speak about the attitudes of many scientists and the general public to psi research in general, and precognition in particular, I often remember a story told by a traveler at the beginning of the century. The traveler decided to surprise the chief of a tribe which had no knowledge of photography. After taking pictures, he told them that he had to use a dark room to develop them. But the chief became angry, "No, do your magic here, in our presence, that we can see it!"

Occasionally, the position of psi research critics remind me of this situation: the phenomena are denied *a priori* by people who do not know the conditions which facilitate the development or manifestation of psi. At the same time, our experience has demonstrated that, like other psi abilities, precognitive abilities (which we term intuitive forecasting) can be successfully trained and developed in quite a large number of individuals.[6,7]

How Exact Are Prophecies?

(Methodology for the Development of Conscious Control of Intuitively Received Precognitive Information)

Barbara Ivanova and Larissa Vilenskaya

(Abstract of the Paper Presented in Absentia at the International Congress on Precognitive Phenomena, *Forecast*–1984, Jerusalem, Israel, December 1983)

In 1972–75 the authors developed an approach for training individuals to bring intuitive (including precognitive) information under their conscious control. The training procedure included: (a) acquaintance with theoretical material concerning these phenomena and abilities, as well as moral and ethical issues relevant to their development and application; (b) relaxation techniques; (c) concentration and visualization exercises; (d) harmonization and creation of a receptive state of mind. Receptive state is a conventional term which actually means creating conditions not for perception of information, but for conscious awareness of the information, since, as a rule, an individual already possesses this information at an unconscious level. Using different approaches, both authors demonstrated that development of other psi abilities facilitates the conscious control of precognitive abilities. Barbara Ivanova found this feature while conducting training in clairvoyance, distant diagnosis and healing, and Larissa Vilenskaya observed a similar phenomenon while carrying out exercises for development of skin vision, aura-diagnosis, and remote perception.

The authors observed that (a) two sensitives can successfully receive the same precognitive information (simultaneously or separately), verifying and complementing each other's results; (b) the highest level of accuracy of psychic precognitive information is about eighty percent, thereby suggesting the existence of an unpredictable (chance) component and of complicated causality/acausality (determinism/non-determinism) relationships in the Universe. This chance element suggests that the ultimate outcome of predictions actually depends on ourselves and our actions.

References

1. Kazantsev, A. *Collective Works*. Vol. 1. Moscow: Molodaya gvardiya, 1977.

2. Zinchenko, V.P., & Leontiev, A.N. "Parapsychology," *Great Soviet Encyclopedia*, Vol. 19, Moscow: Sovetskaya entsiklopediya, 1974, pp. 192–193.

3. Puthoff, H., & Targ, R. "A Perceptual Channel for Information Transfer over Kilometer Distances: Historical Perspective and Recent Research," *Proceedings of the IEEE*, Vol. 64, No. 3, March 1976, pp. 329–354.

4. Pauli, W., & C. J. Jung, (Eds). *The Interpretation of Nature and the Psyche*, (Bollingen Ser. LI). Princeton, N.J.: Princeton University Press, 1955.

5. Lavrov, A.S. "Unexplicable? For the Time Being, Yes," *Smena*, No. 2, 1967, pp. 28–30.

6. Ivanova, B. "Intuitive Forecasting: Experimental and Training Work," *Proceedings of the Second International Congress on Psychotronic Research*, Monte Carlo, 1975, pp. 322–325.

7. Ivanova, B. "Wie man lernt, sich an die Zukunft zu erinnern" (How Can One Learn to Remember the Future?), *Esotera*, Germany, 1977, No. 3, pp. 200-203; No. 4, pp. 296-298 (in German).

How Do Scientists Attempt to Explain Psi?

Barbara Ivanova[*]

In the following selection, Barbara reveals her erudite side, forever intertwining theory, logic, and experience. Developing the philosophy of Soviet biophysicist Alexander Dubrov, Barbara seems to logically deduce explanations for her experiences with healing and remote psychokinesis, as well as her consideration of the role of energy points on Earth. — Eds.

■ In *Phaetians*, one of the most exciting novels by the science fiction writer Alexander Kazantsev,[1] there are several vivid scenes in which inhabitants of the legendary planet Phaeton, by concentrating their will, use their mental powers to operate a relay which opens the massive doors of a mysterious underground chamber. Similarly, in real life we sometimes encounter instances that look more fantastic than fiction. Serious science fiction authors seemingly pick up ideas from the air which often manifest in scientific discoveries and achievements. Although their ideas sometimes seem absurd, they help us to understand and become accustomed to their concrete manifestations.

In this paper we consider some fantastic phenomena and research related to the deliberate control of living and non-living systems by means of particular emanations from the human body. These particular energetic and informational processes are being studied in the Soviet Union and all over the world.

"The Effect of Psychic Energy" is the name of an interesting item by V. Loginov published in the newspaper *Soviet Engineer*.[2] He speaks about bold conclusions "based on theoretical assumptions which, given further favorable development, will be able to explain one of the new mechanisms for error evaluation in the relationships of living systems with their environment. For example, there were

---

[*] This article has been supplemented with additional information by Larissa Vilenskaya. — Eds.

experiments done at the Kirov Polytechnical Institute which, based on preliminary data, support the premise that the neurophysiological condition of the laboratory technician influences the range of physical-mechanical parameters of products made of concrete." The author explains, "We can assume that this effect occurs through the action of the energy which arises during a person's psychic activity and is due to the physiological processes related to this activity."

Included in the article is a reference to the study of our colleague, the Estonian scientist, Tynis Neeme, published in the Proceedings of the First International Conference on Psychotronic Research held in Prague in 1973.[3] It reads: "The sedimentation of suspensions occurs more rapidly in solutions which are acted upon by volitional and emotional concentration." Neeme considers it probable that "a transformation of 'psychic energy' into mechanical, electromagnetic, radioactive, gravitational, and other forms of energy takes place."

The article also mentions Robert Pavlita's work on "psychotronic generators" as well as the experiments conducted by Nina Kulagina and Larissa Vilenskaya on the bio-influence of plant seeds. "The experimental sowing of these seeds showed a difference in the germination between the ordinary seeds and the experimental ones." This is yet more evidence that humans possess a much greater range of possibilities than they are now aware of. They can help plants grow faster with the help of their bioenergy (the name we now give these emanations), and much more, it seems.

A knowledge of the possibilities of bioenergetic fields and their interactions can prove helpful in the most diverse fields and cases. For example, a good worker suddenly begins to perform poorly on the job. Doctors find nothing physically wrong with him, and the man feels himself to be in good health despite his lowered productivity. The supervisor is advised to transfer the man to another position on the conveyer belt because the bio-field of co-workers can often be incompatible. This is also shown by an example where a worker began to suffer when a new man was positioned next to him.

Psychological incompatibility is a well-known fact. But what about bioenergetic incompatibility? Experiments in photographing biological systems in a high-frequency electrical field (the widely known method of Kirlian photography) have demonstrated that in some cases the biofields of two plant leaves or the fingers of two individuals are attracted to each other, while in some cases they are repulsed by the other.[4-7] Perhaps, in the case of bioenergetic incompatibility, the individual's bioenergy is thrown off or expelled in a manner similar to what we see in the photographs. It is possible that these energy radiations and field interactions can in some way influence the quality of products as well as the productivity of workers.

The phenomena and abilities we are interested in (psychic healing, psi information, energetic interactions) are not only important for our everyday lives, but also for a more fundamental understanding of the nature of life and the universe. Our further advanced scientists, who are involved in different problems touching upon psi research, have valid ideas concerning explanations of these phenomena and of their role in living and non-living nature. Among them is the well known biophysicist Dr. Alexander Dubrov, whose primary interest is the influence of geophysical factors (among them the Earth's magnetic field) on living systems. He demonstrated how cosmic factors influence geophysical conditions and determine their activity in time and space. Thus, the geomagnetic field is a link between us and the near part of the cosmos.

Two primary ideas of Dr. Dubrov are: (a) the universal character of the influence of geomagnetic fields; and (b) hypersensitivity of biological systems to electromagnetic fields. The cause is the specific structure of living systems: membrane-structures possessing biological super-conductivity. As is known, all organic and inorganic substances, according to their electric properties, belong to one of the following subgroups: non-conductors (insulators), semi-conductors, conductors, and super-conductors. In Dubrov's opinion, biological membranes can pass electric current without generating a rise in temperature, as in super-conductors, where the current passes without loss. Dr. Dubrov believes that bio-membranes are super-conductors of the second type, where the super-conductor is divided by non-conductors.

All living systems have their own electromagnetic fields, which are as yet insufficiently studied. These fields interact and possibly we can draw energy from them (as we see in the Kirlian photographs). What the Yogis say about the possibility of deriving energy from the Cosmos is not without reason, says Dr. Dubrov. During our healing processes we also utilize this cosmic energy. Our preliminary data indicate that the healing is more thorough in this way, and better than if we use only our bio-energy.

Dubrov said that the magnetic and gravitational fields interact with the magnetosphere of Earth. Through these channels we are linked with our surroundings. From this general reservoir we derive energy, without being aware of the kind of energy it is, and what the processes are which allow us to draw upon it.

This global theory of Dubrov leads us to the following conclusions: when we say that during our healing work cosmic rays are involved, this may have a scientific basis. No less real is the mechanism of the phenomenon: the utilization of the cosmic radiations by the emotionally volitional action of a healer. But it is still not sufficiently explored and not completely clear.

In addition, if the biomagnetism of the healer is connected with the geomagnetic field, we can explain our absent healing processes, performed instantaneously, at any distance—even trans-Atlantically. I receive no less than five to ten telephone healing contacts a day from different towns and countries, which give positive results in varying degrees—up to eighty percent. Physicians are astonished by the force of our influence (which is not diminished at such distances) and give objective proof of the physical changes which occasionally occur immediately, such as the elimination of swellings or tumors. I feel this can be described as "long-distance PK." Dubrov gave a scientific explanation of these facts in his hypothesis of biogravitation; that is, the capacity of living systems to radiate biogravitational fields which penetrate through any screen, at long distances. He wrote:[8]

> From certain data, it may be inferred that a biogravitational field arises in consequence of changes in the conformation of protein structures as a result of the transformations which occur with polypeptide molecules. These changes in conformation induce a strictly ordered, structured crystalline state in the hydrated protein molecules and their oscillations are synchronized, as a result of which a qualitatively new physical situation is established, affecting the atom's symmetry groups and the nature of the sub-molecular space. For this reason, the biogravitational field could equally well (and correctly) be called a "conformational field," the waves could be called "conformation waves" and the wave particles "conformons." The resemblance to traditional conceptions of particle-wave dualism ends here, however, since the

above-mentioned properties of the conformation field also enter into play. Analyzing psi phenomena...we may... conclude that a living organism can be both a receiver and a transmitter of gravitational waves over considerable distances.[8]

Thus, the Dubrov hypothesis explains the "strange" facts of our healing influence at a distance and other related phenomena as the result of the influence of biogravitational field and not as miracles.

Another one of our colleagues among the scientists is Vladimir Neumann, Ph.D. in geology and mineralogy. In his opinion, ancient people could use biogravitational effects for moving heavy stones, e.g., transporting the statues of Easter Island by means of a mysterious energy, *manu*, described by the French ethnographer and archaeologist Francis Masier in his book *Mysterious Easter Island*.[9] He agrees with Prof. Veniamin Pushkin's view that any thinking process which proceeds through the central nervous system, or any image, manner of action, etc., first acquires the form of the hologram,[10] i.e., they create specific energy structures in space.

According to Dr. Neumann,[11] psi phenomena and energies associated with them are closely connected to a structural energy network which functions as a united system at various levels, from galaxies down to even subatomic particles. Within living organisms this structure is associated with the Kenrak-system discovered by Korean scientists and related to acupuncture points and meridians. On Earth this system is represented by the network of forces, triangles and pentangles, connected into an icosahedral-dodecahedral system proposed by Nikolai Goncharov, Valery Makarov, and Vyacheslav Morozov from Moscow.[12] According to this hypothesis, the Earth's nucleus is a crystal shape that possesses crystalline properties, and its force field influences various processes in both the interior and the surface of the Earth. Due to these influences, the Earth can be viewed as a giant crystal (a spherical pentododecahedron combined with a spherical icosahedron), apeces of this complicated crystal being points with particular geological, geomagnetic, and other properties. In the authors' opinion, these major points are centers of some geophysical anomalies (e.g., Kursk magnetic anomaly in the European part of the USSR), as well as centers of ancient civilizations. The researchers mention them as "acupuncture points of the Earth."

In the knots of this network, the researchers assume either a generating or an absorbing energy pulse is being originated and high energy particles are being generated or dispersed. The positive or negative pulse expands along the lines of this network, most likely, as a polarized beam, suggests Dr. Neumann. The frequencies operating here are, as often occurs in nature, the ones typical for natural oscillating circuits (resonance frequencies, i.e., the ones producing effects with minimal energy expenditure and maximal output obtained).

This assumption, says Dr. Neumann, can explain the interactions with the organism and between organisms: it is "co-resonance." The same explains the quasi-independence from space and time in parapsychological contacts. The energy pulses have optional alternative paths, using one of the multiple links of the planetary network (which has not only radial, but spherical components). A polarized beam (ray) which moves on a resonance level through the framework-net of the Earth suffers very little loss of energy at immense distances.

All the above ideas and considerations of open-minded researchers are very fruitful to further promote our understanding of psi and our work in this field.

References

1. Kazantsev, A. *Phaetians*, Moscow: Khudozhestvennaya literatura, 1984 (in Russian).

2. Loginov, V. "The Effect of Psychic Energy, *Soviet Engineer* (the town of Kirov), No. 25, September 4, 1975 (in Russian; English translation in *International Journal of Paraphysics*, Vol. 9, Nos. 4/5, 1975, pp. 105–106).

3. Neeme, T. "On the Presence of Regularity in the Distribution of Indicators of Chemical Tests During Purposeful Volitional and Emotional Concentration of Man at a Close Distance," *Proceedings of the First International Congress of Psychotronic Research*, Vol. 2, Prague, 1973, pp. 152–156.

4. Adamenko, V., "Lightning Takes Photographs," *Nedelya*, No. 43, 1975 (in Russian).

5. "Exploring the Psychobiophysical Reality," *Tekhnika molodezhi*, No. 3, 1980, pp. 50–55 (in Russian; English translation in *International Journal of Paraphysics*, Vol. 14, Nos. 5/6, 1980, pp. 99–105).

6. Vilenskaya, L. "Glowing Phantoms," *Tekhnika molodezhi*, No. 10, 1974 (in Russian; English translation in *The ESP Papers*, S. Ostrander & L.

Schroeder, Eds., New York: Bantam Books, 1976, pp. 173–180).

7. Krippner, S., Rubin, D. (Eds.) *Galaxies of Life: The Human Aura in Acupuncture and Kirlian Photography*, New York: Gordon & Breach, 1973.

8. Dubrov, A.P. "Biogravitation and Psychotronics," *Impact of Science on Society*, Vol. XXIV, No. 4, 1974, pp. 311–319.

9. Masier, F. *Mysterious Easter Island*, Moscow: Mys' Publishing House, 1970 (Russian translation).

10. Pushkin, V. Personal communication, Moscow, 1977.

11. Neumann, V. Personal communication, Moscow, 1978.

12. Goncharov, N., Makarov, V., Morozov, V. "Geo-crystal in the Eyes of Readers," *Tekhnika molodezhi*, No. 1, 1982, pp. 50–52 (in Russian; abridged English translation in *Psi Research*, Vol. 1, No. 2, June 1982, pp. 55–57).

■ IV.
"Exotic" Areas of Psi

Science, if it is set to be renewed, has first of all to be unlimited and thus fearless. Any conventional limitation will be...evidence of wretchedness and thus will become an insuperable hindrance on the way to achievement.

Nicolas Roerich, *Selected Works*, Moscow, 1979

Biological and Physical Approaches to the Problem of Reincarnation: Experiments and Hypotheses

Barbara Ivanova and Larissa Vilenskaya

The following article is the last joint effort of Barbara and Larissa before Larissa's emigration to Israel and later the United States. In it they cite case studies from the Soviet Union which suggest reincarnation and elaborate on their own experiences in regressions.

In the early 1970s, when most American and German researchers conducted reincarnation regressions in deep hypnosis, Barbara developed specific techniques by which individuals might achieve a slightly altered state of consciousness (different from deep hypnosis) which enabled them to experience past life events. The major component of these techniques was an attempt to use healing energies for attaining the regressed state. As a rule, Barbara would put her hands in the shape of her golden chalice, direct the energies in a particular way, and ask out loud for cosmic forces to show the subject impressions of that past life which was most significant for his/her present life and further spiritual development. Many individuals would begin to "see" some strange images, which they would be able to describe in detail. Most people would be certain that they had never seen anything like the images in their present lifetime. These images would not be hallucinatory so much as like a memory or recollection of something almost forgotten, although quite distinct and vivid—what we call "memories of the non-experienced" (i.e., non-experienced in the present lifetime).

We do not regard the results of these tests as hard evidence for reincarnation, since the issue, about which volumes of philosophic, religious, and scientific discussions have been written, is far too complicated to be comprehensively treated in the framework of one brief article. We believe, however, that the innovative approach discussed in the article may be of interest to our readers.—Eds.

111

■ Hundreds of cases proving the reality of the concept of reincarnation are known today in Western[1-8] as well as in Soviet[9-13] publications. Consider the following:

Dima, seven years old, speaks to his grandmother, "Grandma, you will die soon, you know?"

She answers calmly, "Surely, because I'm quite old."

Dima consoles her, "Don't be upset, Granny, I'll die, too, some time."

"O, my God! Don't say such things! You'll live for a long time!" answers the frightened old woman.

"But it doesn't matter that I'll die," says the boy. "Yet, it is a pity that when I die, we'll perhaps never meet again."

"What are you saying, Dima, dear?"

"We are always born again, naturally," explains the little boy. "Only you may turn out to be born in one country and me in another. We may even happen to be born in a different time."

"Where did you get all those silly ideas from? Did someone tell you?"

"No. I just know it. And you know it, too. But we forget all that after some time."

"How can you say such things? You are only seven!"

"Oh, no, Grandma, I'm sixty-seven."

"Silly jokes! Where did you get these ideas from?"

"I can't explain it. But I feel, I just know that it is all true."

This conversation took place on May 20, 1976, in a Moscow family where no one knew of reincarnation. After one of our lectures, the boy's father told us the story.

An article, "The Five-year-old Pianist,"[13] describes a boy, Alyosha, who played as if he was a mature musician. "What piece of music do you like most of all?" he was asked. Alyosha sat down at the piano and began to play with great vigor and passion Beethoven's *Kreyzer Sonata*.

The phenomenon of children who exhibit brilliant talent and knowledge virtually without previous learning, as in the case of "Wunderkinder," can be explained most likely by reincarnation. Similarly, feelings of like or dislike without visible reason, or sudden interest and so on, can also be explained by the concept of reincarnation (which we can simplistically imagine as a continuous chain of lives—the continual rebirth of a human being).

We began to conduct our experiments on depth or remote (that is, incarnational) regressions in 1971. We induced submersions into

112

the past, obtaining information from the subject about his former lives—first of all for educational and practical, i.e., therapeutic or psychotherapeutic purposes. We also pursued purely scientific goals. Our subjects were in normal or light hypnagogic states of mind. In other countries similar experiments using deep hypnosis were also being conducted.

A description of some of our experiments in various periods follows:

1972. During a regression, an ordinary salesgirl, who had very aristocratic features, saw herself wearing silk and velvet. "I have on a very wide puffed skirt, my hands seem to be on my lap, but I do not understand why they are quite high, as if on hoops." While saying this she was sitting with closed eyes, very straight, holding her hands suspended. Obviously, she knew nothing about hoop-skirts (crinolines); otherwise she would not be so surprised.

Children and illiterate people are more ingenuous and possess little knowledge or general information. Therefore, experiments with them result in receiving more reliable scientific data.

1974. A young Spanish-looking lady saw herself in Madrid, Spain, participating in the *corrida*. When she "came back" from her "submersion into deep past," she asked, "What does *toro* mean? Everybody shouted *toro* all the time I was there." The appearance of unknown words from foreign languages unfamiliar to the subjects (which they have certainly never studied), and even whole sentences (xenoglossia or glossolalia) is a frequent occurrence during regression, whether induced or spontaneous.

1977. A woman suffered from pain for many years. The physicians were no help. While in regression she saw her death from a stomach-wound. After the experiment we found on the very place she mentioned an almost invisible light mark on her stomach, resembling a very old scar. However, she had never been wounded (in this life) and she had never noticed this almost invisible spot. It has been stated that scars, birth-marks, or birth defects often appear on the same places as mortal wounds inflicted in the previous incarnations.[1,14] Apparently, the energy element (or the "donors" as some researchers call it) carries over into the new incarnation, i.e., in bodily substances there are traces of the previous existence, as well as other information. In our experiments, as well as experiments of other researchers dealing with reincarnation, we have often been confronted with this phenomenon of so-called pseudo-scars.

After our usual psychotherapeutic post-regression conversation (or super-depth autoanalysis), many pains, paralyses, manias, phobias, and other diseases originating in former existences usually disappear. We have conducted several hundred regressions and the results of some of these cases with their educational and healing implications have already been published.[14-17] A few cases were tape recorded for further analysis and study. The data received seem to be extremely interesting and present starting points for other approaches to the problem. For instance, during the regressions, often a person's mannerisms—gestures, poses, intonations and ways of conversing—suddenly change. A modest man displays self-confidence and an assertive manner, speech and movements. A young man who was a very bad stutterer talked during his regressions for four sessions (each session lasting from half an hour to an hour) and at this time his stuttering scarcely appeared. After our post-regression conversations he practically stopped stuttering. He also became a more serious and spiritually attuned person and began practicing healing after we taught him the method.

It is also possible to submerge into other people's incarnations. We believe that such cases are versions of purposeful or programmed clairvoyance, intuitive retrocognition, or even precognition if we are dealing with future incarnations. We conducted many experiments of this type. Short descriptions of two cases are cited below:

1. The experiment was conducted in Moscow in 1973. Its aim was to detect the previous incarnations of a scientist from Novosibirsk in order to help him with problems he was having. An autosubmersion revealed that in one of his incarnations he was a Hungarian and lived in a border area where people spoke German and Czech. He was imprisoned and later died of suffocation. After this experiment we learned from his son that besides English he had begun to study German, Hungarian and Czech, although the last two languages were of no use to him as a physicist. He was enthusiastic about studying Hungarian and Czech and mastered them easily. We should add that he suffered from asthma and often got severe attacks of asphyxia. These facts were not known to us during our experiment in "regressive incorporation" (complete submersion into another's—or one's own—incarnation). We did not even know who this man was in the photograph which his son showed to us when requesting a consultation.

2. This information was received in 1978 from a woman, one of whose incarnations was studied:

"When I enter a museum where I see paintings made by serfs, my heart is wrung with pity. I imagine that I am one of those people, deprived of all rights, and I suffer. I feel the same when looking at embroidery done by serfs. I turned to Barbara with the request to 'see' who I was in my previous incarnations. She looked somewhere through me and said: 'I see a light-haired serf-girl with a long braid and a sad face. She is wearing a *sarafan* and is sitting on a wooden bench in front of a loom. She is weaving patterns which she created herself. She could not endure slavery and died young.' That impressed me deeply! I am a teacher of painting and drawing, and I gave my students the picture of the serf-girl weaving as an assignment for their exhibition project."

We had many similar cases. We compared the results of our experiments with those of other researchers and analyzed them.[11,14-17]

Another fruitful line of research involves means and possibilities of gathering evidence for the phenomenon of reincarnation by attentive self-observation and by watching other people's activities. We propose that our readers try it. They are sure to observe the so-called spontaneous, or unaccountable gestures, attitudes, and actions which can be logically explained only on the basis of reincarnation. These are remnants or effects of previous lives, or "recollections of the body" (and its energy component). The energy force, released after the disincarnation, seems to become linked with a new-born's body and supplies it with information, including some inappropriate reactions to facts, situations, and conditions which were appropriate in a previous incarnation but are not suitable to the present. For instance, a woman teacher prefers to write or read leaning while over her table, stooping in an inconvenient posture. Where did she acquire this habit? In this life she never used old-fashioned stand-up writing tables. This habit could have developed in a past life.

Another example: a man lifts the tails of his coat when jumping over puddles. Why? They surely won't get wet. But what if he has been a woman wearing long dresses in a former life? Or the case of an old man who always twirls a non-existent beard. Indeed, he never had a beard! Another case: a man cannot bear someone walking close behind him on the street. If this happens, he feels an ache in his back. In the course of regressions we found that in one of his lives he was killed by a shot in the back. He also has a mole on his back resembling a bullet scar. It appeared when the man was twenty-four years old, the very age when the shot was fired in the former life. We would like to emphasize that this information was first received during the "immersion" of another person, who knew nothing about this mini-phobia of the man, nor about the mole. The aches disappeared after a submersion-session and our usual post-regression talk—as have many other fears, psychoses, inexplicable aches, and even dysfunctions of various organs.[6,7,15-17]

Some researchers in the Soviet Union and in the West have recently put forward a number of hypotheses which interpret these phenomena in terms of biology and physics. The authors believe that even the most esoteric phenomena (such as reincarnation) possess underlying physical causes and properties which may manifest themselves at our level of existence, here and now. Certainly such manifestations do not exclude transcendental causes and properties which may appear to occur at another level.

All the hypotheses we know that pertain to the problem of reincarnation can be easily divided into two groups. The first group can be characterized as assumptions of hereditary transfer of information in a broad sense, otherwise known as memory of generations,[11] gene-memory or extra-cerebral memory.[14]

Dr. Isaak Asimov, in his article, "Chemistry and the Human Mind,"[18] reveals that the brain cells contain trillions of minutely different varieties of ribonucleic acid (RNA) and that each RNA molecule can bring about the manufacture of a slightly different protein molecule. His hypothesis is that "every tiny bit of memory present in our brain is a distinctly different...protein molecule." He asks pointedly, "Is recall a matter of 'rifling' through the various molecules and seizing upon the specific one (or ones) associated with that bit of memory?"

Dr. James V. McConnell of the Mental Health Institute of the University of Michigan, adds to this hypothesis the question, "If a change in RNA molecule (or some such) is nature's way of recording memories, can't we go nature one better? Couldn't we synthesize or alter memories in a test tube?"[19]

Dr. George Ungar of the Department of Anesthesiology and Pharmacology at Baylor University College of Medicine reports successful results from the chemical transfer of learned behavior in planarian worms, rats and mice, goldfish and other living organisms. He generated in them absolutely new habits and then examined whether it was possible to single out the new molecules which appeared and to transfer them from the head of one animal into the other. "Although the matter is still largely controversial," Professor Ungar wrote, "more recent work from our laboratory and by other workers leaves no doubt about the reality of the transfer phenomenon."[20] The analysis showed that the isolated "memory substance" is albumen-like. "Natural albumen," Professor Ungar affirms, "contains twenty different amino acids, resembling alphabetical letters. When the brain has to learn something, it has only to join the letters, that is, to make chains of letters as if they were words."[21]

The hypothesis of the existence of a memory substance, though not acknowledged by all researchers,[22] seems, nevertheless, to be very promising for further examination and comprehension of the reincarnation phenomenon. The more so, as the work of the cyberneticist Morris Khvedelidze[23] demonstrated, because DNA (by the agency of which, as is known, the transfer of hereditary information occurs), is preserved in the biosphere. Here the possibility arises that information in the form of specific biomolecules could pass from one organism to another, thus facilitating a memory transfer.

It is worthwhile to cite here the experiments of the Soviet researchers at the Moscow Institute of Molecular Biology.[24] In their experiments the destruction of the RNA-molecules led to the complete disappearance of the specific qualities inherent in these molecules. But when the isolated molecules were drawn together under certain conditions, they reconstituted themselves spontaneously and composed themselves without any external influence on the location of the molecule's fraction in space. Separate parts of them were attracted to each other by the integrative forces of interaction. Thus it was learned that *all the information* required for the reassembly of the molecule is stored in *each separate* part of it. It is obvious that the brain can reconstruct the "memory molecule" even out of its pieces.

The second type of proposed hypothesis pertains to the examination of biofield characteristics, undoubtedly possessed by each individual.[25,26] Such hypotheses imply that after the death of a person his biological field does not disappear, but can exist for a long time in the form of an energy-information complex, which contains all the information about the organism and about the person's life. Among the adherents of this concept is the Soviet researcher Dr. Alexander Romen.[27-29] He wrote, "It is admitted... hypothetically that in the process of the existence of an organism, a specific bioenergy 'image' develops which remains after the organism ceases functioning."[27] Dr. Romen suggests "a possibility of maintaining the personal 'I' (ego)...after death in a definite biological form.... This objective energy image preserves the personal characteristics irrespective of spatial and temporal factors...."[28,29]

A Soviet physicist, Dr. Lev Druzhkin,[30] considers the existence of longitudinal electromagnetic waves that attenuate much slower than ordinary transverse waves and are capable of remaining in space for a long time and of forming a human biofield component. When the biofield spectrum of a living person is similar to that of a dead one, his superconsciousness can perceive the information stored in the biofield of the latter. Afterwards, in the process of contacts established between the superconscious and conscious mind of the living person, the "memory" of events he has never experienced in his life emerges. Such cases have often been described in scientific literature and works of art. It may happen that relatives have similar biofield spectra. Such similarities may also occur between complete strangers. Moreover, an information-bearing biofield (or one of its components, longitudinal electromagnetic waves) spreads over spheres, tangential to the source of radiation.[30] Therefore a living person can perceive this information over a considerable period of time.

It is also possible that the recent hypothesis of Dr. Rupert Sheldrake concerning a specific "morphogenetic field" which underlies nature[31] may shed new light on these phenomena.

All such accumulated evidence and research are widely known in the world today. Some researchers[32,33] believe that facts similar to those described above could be explained in ways other than reincarnation (for instance, by extrasensory perception or the notion of collective unconscious postulated by Carl Jung). Nevertheless, the results of reincarnation research deserve serious attention and further study from many perspectives. One important aspect concerns its moral and ethical consequences, which should be analyzed in detail and comprehensively. It is also very important to consider the beneficial influence this knowledge can have upon people, provided they develop an appropriate attitude toward the

119

concept. It is additionally necessary to establish connections between ancient traditions and modern scientific hypotheses and ideas: such integrated knowledge is very important for the development of our society and even for our whole civilization.

References

1. Stevenson, I. "Twenty Cases Suggestive of Reincarnation," *Proceedings of the American Society for Psychical Research*, Vol. 26, September 1966.

2. Stevenson, I. "Some New Cases Suggestive of Reincarnation," *Journal of the American Society for Psychical Research*, Vol. 68, No. 1, 1974, pp. 58–90.

3. Andrade, H. *Caso Ruytemberg Rocha*, Monograph No. 1, Department of Science at the Brazilian Institute of Psychobiophysical Research, São Paulo, Brazil, 1971 (in Portuguese).

4. Passian, R. *Abschied ohne Wiederker? Erlebtes—Erfahrenes—Erforschtes*. Pforzheim: R. Fischer Verlag, 1973 (in German).

5. Ruth, R. *Reincarnation and Science*. New Delhi, 1973.

6. Dethlefsen, T. *Das Leben nach dem Leben. Gespräche mit Wiedergeborenen*. München-Wien: C. Bertelsmann Verlag, 1974 (in German).

7. Dethlefsen, T. *Das Erlebnis des Wiedergeburt. Heilung durch Reinkarnation*. München-Wien: C. Bertelsmann Verlag, 1976 (in German).

8. Klausner, M. "Different Ways to Remember Past Impressions," in *Proceedings of the Second International Congress on Psychotronic Research*, Monte Carlo, 1975, pp. 341–344.

9. Baba-Zade, I. "Mystery of a Little American," *Moskovsky komsomolets*, December 15, 1968 (in Russian).

10. Stepanyants, M. *Lotus on the Palms: Notes on a Spiritual Life in India*, Moscow: Nauka, 1971, pp. 33–34 (in Russian).

11. Vilenskaya L., Ivanova B. "I Remember as it Was Some 1,000 Years Ago," *Volzhsky komsomolets* (city of Kuibyshev), October 11, 1975 (in Russian).

12. Goulmen, D. "On the Threshold of a Mystery," *Literaturn ya gazeta*, May 31, 1978 (in Russian).

13. Druzhnikov, A. "The Five-year-old Pianist," *Vechernyay Moskva*, January 28, 1978 (in Russian).

14. Ivanova, B. "Reencarnation: su base fisiologica y biologica," *C nocimento de la nueva Era*, No. 441, Buenos Aires, September 1974 (in Spanish).

15. Passian, R. "Erziehung durch Erinnerungen an Frühere Leben. Neue Methoden und Anwedungsberieche der Reinkarnationsforschung. Interview mit der russischen Parapsychologin Barbara Ivanova," *Esotera*, July 1974 (in German).

16. Ivanova, B. "Reincarnaation ja parantaminen," *Ultra* , No. 9, 1975 (in Finnish).

17. Gris, H., & Dick, W. *The New Soviet Psychic Discoveries*. New York: Warner Books, 1979, pp. 168–183.

18. Asimov, I. "Chemistry and the Human Mind," *Span*, Vol. VIII, No. 10, October 1967, p. 42.

19. McConnell, J. "Cannibals, Chemicals, and Contiguity," *Animal Behavior*, Supplement 1, reprint (n.d.), p. 61 (cited in [5]).

20. Ungar, G. "Transfer of Learned Behavior by Brain Extracts," *Journal of Biological Psychology*, Vol. IX, No. 1, June 1967, p. 12.

21. "The Substance, of Which Thoughts are Made," *Literaturnaya gazeta*, May 21, 1975 (in Russian).

22. Livanov, M., Vinogradova, O., Rozanov, S. "Dubious Substance, Erroneous Ideas," Ibid.

23. Khvedelidze, M. "Does the Energo-Informational Dualism Mean the Equivalence of Mutual Transformations of Energy and Information in Living Systems?" *Izvestiya akademii nauk gruzinskoy SSR*, Series Biology, Vol. 1, No. 4, 1975, p. 325 (in Russian).

24. *New Scientist*, May 1974, p. 329.

25. Karagulla, S. *Breakthrough to Creativity: Your Higher Sense Perception*. Santa Monica, Ca.: De Vorss, 1967.

26. Yarovoy, Y. "Biological Energy Field: Fiction or Reality?" *Ural*, No. 5, 1970, p. 138.

27. Romen, A. "On Some Aspects of Bioenergetics," in *Some Questions of Biodynamics and Bioenergetics of the Organism in Norm and Pathology, Biostimulation by Laser-Irradiations*, Materials of the First Republican Conference, May 1971. Part II, Alma-Ata, 1972, pp. 44–47 (in Russian).

28. Romen, A. "Psychoenergetics in Theoretical and Practical Aspects," in *Proceedings of the Third International Congress on Psychotronic Research*, Tokyo, 1977.

29. "Third International Congress on Psychotronic Research," *International Journal of Paraphysics*, Vol. 11, Nos. 3/4, 1977, p. 55.

30. Druzhkin, L., Vilenskaya, L. "On the Physical Nature of Bioinformation Signals," unpublished manuscript.

31. Sheldrake, R. *A New Science of Life: The Hypothesis of Formative Causation*. Los Angeles: J.P. Tarcher, 1981.

32. Krippner, S. *Human Possibilities: Mind Exploration in the USSR and Eastern Europe*, Garden City, N.Y.: Anchor Press, 1980, pp. 207–208.

33. Murphy, G. "A Caringtonian Approach to Ian Stevenson's *Twenty Cases Suggestive of Reincarnation*," *Journal of the American Society for Psychical Research*, Vol. 67, 1973, pp. 117-129.

Reincarnation and Healing

Barbara Ivanova

In the following discussion of the healing aspects of "reincarnation" regressions which give information about possible past lives, Barbara offers insights into her own processes of mental imagery and healing. She elucidates how such regressions can provide practical suggestions for assistance with a present-day difficulty or negative pattern.—Eds.

■ In my healing work I use not only bioenergy but psi information received from "other dimensions," as described by Denis Kelsey and Joan Grant in their splendid work *Many Lifetimes*.

I now prefer to heal at a distance, using telephone calls as a means of feedback. The "healees" are often individuals whom I do not know and have never seen. When such a call arrives, I can "see" (using the technique of receiving quasi-visual effects) the person and the illness, but also the previous incarnations. (We know that it is not so simple as previous since the incarnation process is deep and complicated, and our concepts of space and time are far from being sufficiently complete to clearly delineate between then and now.)

The following are examples of reincarnational sources of illnesses so we can understand how previous incarnations work on the individual here and now.

At one time I had a call from a plain village woman, whom had never seen before. She complained of pains, stiffness, a coldness in her body, primarily in her neck, shoulders, and hip She had suffered many years, and no one could help her. Gradua I got the vision of a young and finely delicate aristocratic girl in Italian palace. I described the features of the girl, and the wom said that it was *her* face! In fact, friends have called her "madonn all of her life! I could not have known this nor described her prese appearance by ordinary, logical means.

In the first scene the girl was kneeling in prayer. In the second vision I "saw" her fastened on her wrists to a stone wall, in a medieval cellar. The wall was cold and damp, and she was chilled all over. I "worked" on the situation, "removed" it, and the scene changed: they took her into a kind of bed (of a type I had never seen before) near a fireplace. Immediately the woman on the phone said that she was feeling better—but, curiously, only on one side. It was the side which was near the fire in my quasi-visual scene! She could not have known it, since I did not say a word about the vision. I only asked her how she was feeling.

Afterwards I covered her in my mental "picture" with a torn blanket (although I did not program the blanket to be torn). Immediately she said that she was well and the coldness had vanished. We needed two or three such conversations on the telephone, and she has been well now for almost a year. The illness did not appear again. She does not know my proceedings, since I did not explain the process to her. She would neither understand, nor believe it, and I did not want to frighten her.

Another case concerns a young man with nervous troubles. He had been treated as mentally ill and believed he was. But we know that many so-called mental illnesses are remnants of impressions and actions from other incarnations. (For example, claustrophobia may be caused by having been locked up in a small prison cell for a long time, or having died there, in one of our many lifetimes. Or the fear of heights can appear after having been pushed down from a high rock to one's death.) I tried to find out what his trouble was.

Through the mechanism of our trained clairvoyance awakening, I received the psi information that he had been a French officer in one of his incarnations and was killed with a sabre. I mentioned the places of his body where the weapon entered and left his body, and then I forgot the case. The next day his mother telephoned me and said in a very excited voice, "The boy has birthmarks—exactly on the places which you indicated—like very pale, almost invisible scars of sabrewounds.... But he has never had wounds there!" From my articles she knew the opinion of H.N. Banergee, Hernani Andrade, and Ian Stevenson that on the places where mortal wounds were inflicted in previous incarnations we often find birthmarks or genetic deformities.

After such revelations the person is generally much calmer or totally well. The process works like the psychoanalytical method, only tuned into the deeper layers of the individual-formation.

The best way we have found to assist in reincarnational healing is to regress patients to their past lives, so they can experience these again first-hand. We carried out many such experiments (see the description of some of them in the previous article), that worked generally well.

In recurrent dreams we often experience our own death in one of our previous incarnations, and are troubled by the dream until it is understood. Then it vanishes and we are calm and undisturbed once again. The same is true with other past life (extra-cerebral) memories. Many important conclusions can be derived from dreams, including our future acts or attitudes (if we understand how to use this form of psi information), possibilities for mental and physical healing, moral changes, or cleansing from negative feelings and deeds.

For example, a woman once told me about a recurrent dream which greatly troubled her and made her nervous. In the dream she was on railroad tracks as a train was approaching, yet she did not move despite her tremendous fear and terror. Today, when face to face with difficulties, her pattern is to avoid them, rather than to fight. I helped her to "see" this incarnation, and the suicidal situation. Because she thought that she could not master this situation and her difficulties, she did not fight. Now she makes the same mistake of surrendering on life's battlefield, again and again! And the type of difficulty is always the same. She had to understand that suicide, as every form of avoiding decision, is not a way out of problems—we must eventually solve them anyway! And if we do not solve them in this lifetime, they appear again and again, in different forms and situations, in our present life, and in the next ones—until we learn to master them in the right way.

I asked her if she had a scar across her body, over the stomach. She said that she had something like a scar—but she had never received a wound at this spot! This was the same place I "saw" the fatal wound under the wheels of the train. Her moods changed radically after this experiment and she became stronger as a person and more cheerful. Following her regression and my explanation of the influence of past existences, as well as her own efforts to change her attitudes, the dark, recurrent dream did not appear again.

There are many different reincarnational causes for fears and phobias. For example, one of my friends did not like cats and feared them. She panicked when she saw a cat! I had a flash and said, "In one of your incarnations you were murdered by a black panther."

She cried, "How do you know about my recurrent dream? I often see a terrible giant black cat, attacking me—killing and eating me! What a coincidence!"

But it was not a coincidence. It was her far-memory progressing into her present dreams, which I could also "see." After this conversation and my explanations, her attitude toward cats changed and the dream did not appear again. And she was calmer, in general. Thus, reincarnational healing works in many different forms.

Following extensive experimentation, we believe that it is very important to understand the facts of reincarnation, the purpose of far-memory flashes, and their influence on us. With the help of this understanding, we can change our life and our entire being for the best, and so change the fate of humankind, and our collective karma which threatens to lead us to a holocaust.

A Linguistic Approach to the Problem of the "Voices from the Unknown"

Barbara Ivanova

The phenomenon of voices on tape occurs when questions are asked while an audiotape is recording, and the room is kept silent as the tape continues to record during the "answer" period. When the tape is replayed, during the answer phase voices and sounds are heard on the tape. Some have been deciphered by researchers including Friedrich Jürgenson from Sweden, Konstantin Raudive from Germany and Alexander MacRae from Scotland, while other utterances remain too garbled to discern verbal communication (for more detailed information, see the book *Breakthrough: An Amazing Experiment in Electronic Communication with the Dead* by Raudive, published by Colin Smythe, Gerralds Cross, England, in 1971, and the article "Some Findings Relating to the Electronic Voice Phenomenon" by MacRae in the March 1984 issue of *Psi Research* journal).

Barbara here explores this phenomenon and its possible relationship to "other spatial or temporal dimensions"; that is, extra-terrestrials. Although such a viewpoint is highly controversial, and, for the time being, no one has presented decisive evidence which would confirm it at the same time we are also lacking evidence to deny it. Therefore, we feel that an open-minded approach is the best we can offer. — Es.

Since I am a linguist by education and was a teacher of languages before I became a parapsychologist, I am offering here a linguistic explanation for the voices on tape peculiarities. This phenomenon was partially presented at the congress on the voices phenomenon in 1977 (in my paper read in absentia and published in the book *Voci dall' invisibile* (Voices from the Invisible) [Milan: Armenia Edittore, 1978].

This book described audiotapes on which not only human voices were recorded, but other sounds as well: music, moans, sounds of steps, car-collisions, skirmishes, etc., which apparently demonstrate future or past events and can be identified, as they sometimes were. This fact gives us a hint about the possibility of contacts with other spatial or temporal dimensions.

The dialogues which the voice-investigator, Fr. Jürgenson, and others obtain on tapes show us clear words and meanings. However, when the communications are not in these clear-cut forms, but in the usual confusion of norms and languages, then it could be a "language-code-reconstruction contact."

In one of the best Russian science-fiction books, *Chas byka* (The Hour of the Ox), written by one of our favorite science-fiction writers, Ivan Efremov, cosmonauts approach an unknown planet and decode the language of its population with the help of a special technique. More or less the same is described in many books, all over the world. The existence of such a method cannot be excluded. But in reconstructing a language, no computer can correctly reflect all the peculiarities, fine shades, hues, nuances, stylistics, phonetics, historical meanings, and other traits or outlines. That could well be the reason for archaic forms, dialect expressions, and distorted sentence-constructions appearing on the tapes, which are not typical of the geographic place or the historical time. They are not in the form of here and now, nor of any place or time on our planet. The technical computer-decoding of our terrestrial languages could well account for such mixtures and distortions. This lack of precision in the language forms of the voices is logical, since the reconstruction technique includes many intricate factors.

There can be two decoding systems:

(a) a synchronous cut, which includes all the languages of the planet, reconstructing them simultaneously, in their present state, with all the dialects and variations, as if cutting the whole language system horizontally—if the decoders think that we have only one main language in our world;

(b) a diachronous cut, vertical, through all times; that is, penetrating into the historical development of one language or branch of languages. The sentences of this kind, which appear on the tapes, are situated between the limits of a language, including all its stages and processes of development—all forms of its past and present.

Both reconstruction methods can appear mixed together. In such cases the sentences on the tapes include words and grammatical, phonetic variations, which do not exist as a norm anywhere on the Earth, and have never existed in such combinations. Only the separated components can exist now—or could be traced in the past. The decoders, logically, can neither know nor feel it. They create an artificial imitation, a type of a meta-language.

But who are "they"? We cannot exclude the probability of interference by beings from other planets. In the USSR the possibility of the existence of extraterrestrial civilizations (as well as some means of contact with them) is not ignored and is investigated on the highest scientific levels.[*] I myself participated in three "semiclosed," as we call it (that is, not openly known in the mass media and with more or less limited participation), conferences of such a type:

(a) 1974—at the Ninth Conference, dedicated to the development of the scientific ideas of Konstantin Tziolkovsky, in the town of Kaluga (his birthplace). He was a famous scientist who was centuries ahead of his time—a type of "messenger from the future," as we say. I presented a brief speech at the section, "Problems of Cosmic Medicine and Biology," about our work in "cosmos-bio-energy influence" (our method of healing, introduced in the USSR by parapsychologist Larissa Vilenskaya and myself in 1972).

(b) 1975—participation at the Tenth Conference, in the same town of Kaluga, where I was invited to speak at the symposium, "Man will not eternally stay on the Earth," as Tziolkovsky postulated. I gave a brief description of the area of intuitive information (as I denominate clairvoyance in all its forms and expressions)—which could help humankind to find a suitable and acceptable planet with good conditions, should some (geological or social) factors force us to leave our planet. I gave as an example the psychic probe of Mercury, carried out by the famous psychics Harold Sherman and Ingo Swann, confirmed later by Mariner-10. also to d ... o t ur vo k in ay 1 74 75 e er in ntal d t ing oup or ir ui ve pr gr sis nd l ng -dist ce age ign s.

(1 75 — t t e T eore ical Co erer , " n a Co os," held t t e or or sso Mo co Un ers I s ke a he s ion, "F rol ler s f or acts ith Ex rate stri Civ atic ," w ere I p stu at d ha n w, t ou l w t hni le ou plan can es ab ish th c nt ct o y ir a arap ch gic ay

---

[*] Soviet mass media, however, often does not reflect these investigations. On the contrary—virtually the only publications are negative.

[**] This method may be proven to be quick and inexpensive, while also providing all the needed information. Yet, it does not exclude other, technological ways.

It is possible that representatives of some civilizations from other planets, perhaps from many of them, are here among us already. Who knows for how many centuries. And there are many possibilities of their mimicry and camouflaging forms of existence here, as well as means for us to learn about them. I enumerated some of the traits, by which, in my opinion, we could distinguish them (e.g., spiritually-looking faces, kindness, altruism, non-acceptance of violence in any form, sincere love and protection of animals and all living creatures). I believe that most of them are not only observers here, but help us on our way to real development. Perhaps they are—and have been for a long time—in constant contact with many people and interfere positively in some areas of the scientific and social life of our planet through different means. One of these forms of influencing and contacting us might well be the voices on tape.

It is quite possible that they are trying many technical ways to be understood by us, and prepared this one—the bridge, as they call it—among others. We occasionally catch these voices on our tapes—when their forms of life and existence, or situation, or some other (technical or psychological) factors, which we are unable to know or understand now, do not allow them to communicate with us in other, more direct forms.

This is only one way of understanding the voices' origin. It is connected with the idea of physical multi-dimensionality. Who can deny the possibility of existence of planet systems in other space-dimension variations? Or of beings, "locally" near us, but in other —energetic rather than physical and substantial—forms of life. Perhaps, coming from other space and time configuration-worlds, or forms of life, they master the physical phenomena which we (or our apparatus) are able to perceive. It is not absolutely necessary that their "language-decoding" computer (which some of us imagine as a huge iron thing with many wires) is exactly as we think it to be. In the early days, our tape recorders were also big monsters —and still will be different later on, not only in size, but in many other aspects. Perhaps they will be in a form of matter which we still do not now perceive nor detect.

I do not want to contradict the opinion of Fr. Jürgenson and others—I respect and agree with it. But it is important to show other alternatives and possible explanations. Not to exclude theirs, but to amplify the lines of understanding, and to give other clues and possible ways of investigation (other than simply formulae and numbers) to realize this reality: the origin and purposes of the voices phenomena and other para-facts. Both lines can coexist. They will help people who cannot grasp and accept the reality of "life after life" to observe and approach such real facts, not to deny them *a priori*, but to work with them. This will be a good step forward for many individuals.

Human beings are the principal instruments and implements of knowledge. And we have to understand our mutual psychological evolution (or even revolution) toward general positive changes on the planet, toward moral and ethical elevation. Every step of this understanding is important for all of us. This is our main purpose and goal, the only meaning and justification of our existence.

■ V.

The Inherent Link in Living Nature

A Plea

The wounded bird wouldn't come to me,
The wounded remained afraid.
This old nightmare keeps returning:
A wounded bird lies trembling on the blood-soaked grass.

REFRAIN: The birds, fish and beasts
Gaze into our human souls.

People, spare them,
Do not kill them in vain.

For the sky is not the sky without birds,
The sea not the sea without fish,
The land is not land without beasts!

People, you are giants, colossi,
You have guns, nets, and traps;
You are fearless and have infinite power.
You must also have hearts, human hearts.

REFRAIN: Humans, peoples of the earth, nations,
We are in nature's debt forever.
We've got to pay this debt off somehow —
And let that wounded bird spread its wings.

Robert Rozhdestvensky

*Barbara Ivanova healing by telephone. In her
meditation, she sends healing energy and feels herself
united with all other living creatures in the world.*

Nature Is One World

Barbara Ivanova

Building upon experiments of Cleve Backster and Dr. Veniamin Push-kin concerning interspecies communication with plants, Barbara explores her belief that nature is but one single being. In nature, she contends, animal, vegetable, mineral, and human realms unite, affect and are interdependent upon one another. — Eds.

■ Most of us remember the old fairy tale about a courageous young man who dared a dangerous adventure in order to save his beloved lady, who had been captured by a witch. Along the way, he helped everyone who needed his help: the branch of a tree was broken, and he used clay to fix it and to help it to heal; a bird accidentally sprained its wing, and he healed it as would a good doctor; a fish swallowed a sharp stone and was left helpless out of water, and he helped it to free itself from the stone and return to water. Afterward, the animals and plants paid him with kindness for his kindness, and saved him from all the troubles he encountered on his journey.

This fairy tale is told in many countries and on all continents, but everywhere differently. In all versions of this tale, the hero is a poor but good hearted person. Suddenly an antagonist appears who seeks riches, a life without troubles and problems, and opportunities to govern everyone and everything. This antagonist would not hesitate to command any unbounded deeds to achieve his goal. He would never stop to help a flower or animal which was caught in a trap, or a fish return to water. Consequently, plants and living creatures return the same favor when he encounters troubles in any way, no one will help him. Quite the contrary, they create artificial difficulties for him, and he is unable to reach his goal.

We must ask why all these aspects of fairy tales are so similar although they were composed by different people, who live far from one another and have no connections between them. This question can be answered traditionally with another question: are these more than simply fairy tales? Most likely, these are symbols

which tell of an inherent, inseparable link between all living creatures, and of all three worlds: the inanimate world, the vegetable
kingdom, and the animal kingdom.

When I learned of the most interesting experiments of psychologist Dr. Veniamin Pushkin (see the article "Flower, Answer!" in
Znanie-Sila, No. 11, 1972), which are a continuation and expansion
of Cleve Backster's well known experiments in the field of communication between plants, this interconnection and link became more
clear. If a flower can perceive everything—human emotions, our
thoughts and desires—and not only receive but also evaluate them
(as in the cases when plants reacted to the death or illness of their
owner, to murder, or even to the breaking of an egg), then where
is the borderline between the possible and impossible? Obviously,
something exists which links together all living beings. It would
seem that the old belief that if one presses his/her back to the trunk
of a tree and asks it for help, one can be invigorated and receive
energy, appeared not by chance. This phenomenon is symbolized
by the legend about the ancient hero Antaeus who gained his
power from the Mother-Earth and who died only when he was
separated from the Earth.

A most interesting adventure along the way of scientific development in our civilization is a trip to the world of living cells,
into the world of so-called primitive systems. The newspaper
Moskovskaya pravda, on November 2, 1972, published an article by
Tass reporter A. Presnyakov, "Light Signals of Living Cells." The
author described the officially registered discovery of Soviet scientists Vlail Kaznacheyev, Semen Shurin, and Ludmila Mikhailova,
who demonstrated that two biological systems reliably separated by
a transparent crystalline plate are capable of interacting with one
another through electromagnetic signals in the ultraviolet range.
This provides much interesting evidence. At present, the Kirlian
effect (high-frequency photography) can also assist researchers in
detecting minute changes in the condition of plants, animals and
humans. Using Kirlian photography, one can observe a multi-
colored world of radiations emitted by all living beings. When a
plant is injured or when an individual experiences strong emotions,
the regular blue emissions often change to orange and red protu-
berances.

Are these perhaps the signals which each living being can send
in a critical situation to the surrounding world? Can a living cell
perhaps inform other cells of its "well-being"? Can one living

organism inform another living organism? Can one individual silently call another individual for help? Nature is one world, and, in this sense, if we harm another living being, we harm ourselves as well. The world would be a much better place to live if all of us might remember this simple, eternal rule of life.

Barbara Ivanova's cat, Yashka

Our Friends and Saviors:
Psi in Animals*

Barbara Ivanova

In this anecdotal account, Barbara explores her concept of "The Law of Unselfish Love" as seen in the behavior of animals and pets. In the often extraordinary degrees of unconditional love seen in animals, Barbara finds a model for human relationships with the whole of nature. — Eds.

■ A Soviet journal *Nauka i Zhizn'* carries a regular column under the heading "Our Smaller Brothers." In Number 12 of 1975, a story entitled "My Life-Savior" described a very interesting case which illustrates (along with thousands of other cases) that animals have a faculty of precognition and are sometimes able to use it volitionally to rescue people. In brief, a certain tom cat, Smoke, returned home early one evening after only half an hour of meandering, rather than his habitual full night of adventures. During the night, Smoke did not let his master sleep. Several times he woke his master and made him go to the door as if asking to be let out. And then Smoke would not leave, but instead sat in the doorway and meowed desperately. Finally, as his master went to bed again, Smoke meowed loudly and tried to pull off the bed-covers. This clearly indicated that one way or another, he wanted to get his master out of bed and the house. The man, thinking, "What is the matter with this cat?" finally got up and followed the cat to the door again. Suddenly, there was a loud noise, and a very large portion of plaster from the ceiling fell on the pillow and covered it completely.

Clearly, serious damage would have occurred to the man if he had not followed his pet's calling. And as far as Smoke was concerned? The cat, which had exposed himself to danger by

---

* The extended version of the article by Barbara Ivanova, "Psi in Animals," has been published in *Metascience Quarterly (A New Age Journal of Parapsychology)*, Vol. 1, No. 3, Autumn 1980.

remaining around the bed to call his master and to pull the covers off—now looked at the bed, at the ceiling, the master, and then nonchalantly walked through the door and out into the night. He had nothing more to do in the house for the moment. Thus ends the story and the column. "Coincidence," you say? There are definitely too many coincidences. And not only with cats.

On October 10, 1976, *Izvestiya*, a national Soviet newspaper, published an article entitled, "Mysteries in the World of Animals." The following question was put to the readers, "If you throw a stone into the river and your dog finds it and brings it back, how can he find the exact stone underwater? How can he use his sense of smell there?... The dog has to be guided by a still unknown 'sixth sense' for orienting underwater," writes the author. He then relates other cases of dogs finding their way in an unknown terrain, running hundreds of kilometers through woods and towns, etc.

In the book *Operatsiya "Ch"* ("Operation 'Ch,'" Moscow, 1976), written by B. Ryabinin, there is an essay on "Accuracy in Finding Directions and Fidelity." Many case histories are given which illustrate a synchronicity of the time and moment of illnesses and deaths of dogs and when their masters, who were very far away, would become ill and die. One specific case described a dog that became ill and would not eat for three days during which time it lay in a doorway and periodically howled with tears rolling from its eyes. Following this period, the dog became well and resumed its normal behavior. Two days later, the family got the following news: the dog's master had been involved in an airplane accident, was unconscious for six hours, and literally spent two days at death's door. At the exact moment when the hospitalized master was being operated upon and died—the dog began its howling. The dog also began howling again when the funeral began many miles away. "Coincidences?"

Ryabinin's book describes a truly dramatic occurrence. A dog belonging to one of Napoleon's soldiers was lost in Russia and ultimately wound up finding his master after traveling for a year and a half. The dog had to pass through a part of Russia, all of Poland, Germany, and a part of Italy and France! There were rivers, towns, woods, and many dangers and difficulties. One of the most noteworthy difficulties was that the village where the master ended up living after the war was one to which the dog had never been!

This case is well-documented and has been described many times. Most people have heard about such situations with dogs. But cats, too, have been known to demonstrate the ability, fidelity and will for finding their masters. There is a story about Lisa, the cat who walked over 600 kilometers during one wintry month to find her way back home. She was taken from home inside of a basket on a train, and could not have "remembered" the way. In another case a cat came 1,250 kilometers home in one month!

Horses have also demonstrated direction-finding abilities. In 1944 an entire herd of horses was transported by train from Mongolia to Kazakhstan. On a rainy day the horses were left alone in a meadow, and soon disappeared. Three days later they were all stopped by frontier guards at the border of Mongolia.

There are even cases involving wolves. Prof. P. Manteufel described a tame wolf that was transported in a box in a closed car from the Moscow Zoo to be displayed at a conference about animals. The wolf escaped from the conference, but he ran directly back to the zoo and into his cage.

Ryabinin's essay illustrates the "Law of Unselfish Love." Dogs save small children by carrying them out of a house some moments before the roof comes crashing down. Many dogs have been known to sense the imminence of earthquakes and to save people by leading them out of dangerous areas. Wise men in villages, who trust in animals and their abilities to foresee events, have often been able to predict earthquakes and avalanches and to act accordingly, thus helping to save others as well. Nonbelievers perished. For many dogs that have risked their lives by staying in a dangerous area instead of running away, the "Law of Unselfish Love" has often proved stronger than the will to live. Why do the animals sacrifice themselves? What is this Law?

A woman who was a teacher and a former colleague of mine told me the following story: she was living in a village one summer and found it necessary to go to another one. It was a long walk and on the way two large black dogs joined her, which she found good company. At one point it was necessary to cross a river. Suddenly, while on the bridge, the dogs would not allow her to continue across the bridge. She tried everything she could to dissuade them, to frighten them away, but they simply stood in her way and would not let her cross the bridge. Finally she gave up and returned home. The next day she was told that a party of drunkards in the forest on the other side of the bridge (which she had been unable to cross, because of the strange behavior of the dogs) had committed some crimes of molestation. The rapes had occurred literally minutes after the time when her two canine companions had prevented her from crossing the river. The dogs had definitely protected her, and possibly even saved her life. But how could they have "known"? And what caused them to behave in such a manner?

Even rats can indicate a danger. It is common knowledge that rats leave a doomed ship. Here is an interesting story: the owner of an old ship decided to sink it and collect the insurance on it. But he was unable to hire sailors for this last voyage because they had all seen rats leaving the ship! How could the rats have known about the owner's mental decision-making process? This psi quality, prescience, regarding future dangers is necessary to any living being during the process of survival and evolution of the species.

I. Zayanchkovsky wrote an article entitled, "Animals as Sinoptics (weather-forecasters)" which was published in a collection of essays *Na sushe i na more* ("On Land and Sea," Moscow, 1973). He describes very interesting facts which detail how animals feel and forecast weather changes, natural calamities, etc. In 1902, a glowing cloud of gas shot up from a volcanic crater on the island of Martinique. In the course of thirty seconds, the entire town of Saint Pierre was immolated. Eventually, beneath the ruins of the town were found the charred remains of thirty thousand people and only one, single corpse of a small cat. As it turned out, long before the eruption of the volcano occurred, all the birds flew away from the town. Then serpents and other reptiles abandoned the town. Finally, dogs, cats and other animals fled. If the people of the doomed town would have known about and possibly had believed in this type of animal intuition or clairvoyance, they might not have perished.

A friend from the city of Riga told me that from the moment he acquired a very dangerous illness in his legs, his little dog slept exactly on his sore legs, sat on his lap all day long, and literally clung to the legs. The dog died after a month. The master felt better and despite medical diagnoses and opinions, the illness disappeared. At times when I have experienced pain or some other stresses, my cat, Yashka, has resisted the apparently universal and instinctive demands to flee impending danger. Like other animals who have expressed unselfish love by facing danger or death to assist or rescue their human friends, Yashka has repeatedly demonstrated a type of self-sacrifice that few human beings evince. If my knees hurt, he sleeps on them until they are well; if it is my heart, he insists on sleeping near it; the same with my hands and any other spot—in spite of all my efforts not to permit it. Cases like this are well known among pet "owners." (I do not like this expression—how can one living being be the "owner" of another one? It seems to me a monstrous thing!)

How can we explain all of this? Even birds, butterflies, fish, and other creatures are sometimes reported to find their way. Instinct? But what is instinct? A word, not an explanation. How does instinct of this type operate?

Let us take the concept of the biological clock which functions in people, animals, and even in plants (which "go to sleep" and close their leaves at exact times which are typical for a given plant). All living beings seem to be marvelous autoregulating and self-restoring cybernetic systems which work much better than even the most sophisticated systems created by humans.

As we know, human beings are animals too, and we would not have survived until now without this type of intuition. But here is another side of the problem: we would be, perhaps, less human were it not for the "Law of Unselfish Love" and the examples of it that our animal brethren continue to demonstrate to us, through all of history. We say now, "The dog has humanized man." The same is true for other animals. They not only help us and occasionally save us by using their psi-faculties, but they continue to educate and humanize us in many senses. Families which have animals are generally a much greater pleasure to visit and to know. They become more sensitive and kind-hearted, less aggressive and selfish. Daily contact with any of our animal brethren of Nature makes us more worthy of being called Human.

With Love to Animals and Humans

An Interview with Keith Harary

When our friend, psychologist Keith Harary, author (together with physicist Russell Targ) of *The Mind Race: Understanding and Using Psychic Abilities* (New York: Villard Books, 1984) traveled to Moscow in September 1983, we gave him the telephone number of Barbara Ivanova and asked him to visit her and to convey our regards, with the hope that he would be fortunate enough to know this wonderful individual. After returning from Moscow, Keith was kind enough to grant us an interview and shared with us his impressions of meeting with Barbara. And we, in turn, decided to share them with our readers. —Eds.

■ I spent only one day with Barbara, but I enjoyed it very much. I think she is a *very* bright woman, and things are often difficult for bright women—in this country, too. I think she's been through a lot of hardship, but underneath that (and not very far underneath it) there is an incredible warmth, a very real feeling of compassion. She also has a strong sense of purpose. She feels that she is to share in a very special side of human reality, and this comes across to the people around her, who also feel the purpose. There is a lot of concern and respect for her among the people around her—she is a teacher. They truly care about her and about what she is doing.

She is a very compassionate, warm, emotive kind of person, and you get a lot of feeling from her. There is no doubt, however, that she's really been through hard times. Her friends are afraid for her because she is rather non-traditional in her viewpoints—she would be non-traditional over here too! None of what she's done is political, as far as I understand, at least not directly; it is more spiritual and scientific. She focuses on this unexplored part of ourselves—what does it mean, let's look at it, it's important.

Barbara tries to look at the human potential side of psi. While the majority wonders, "What kind of application can we get from this?" she is convinced that when people see that the applications work, they begin to understand their own potential. Since in the Soviet Union the application is what everyone talks about, we have to elaborate on the fact that these applications imply that there is something here which has human potential capabilities. Athough many of the scientists whom we met in the USSR were thinking about applications, many were also thinking about the implications in human potential. I believe Barbara is explicitly thinking about what this means for human beings. The scientific community starts with applications and moves toward human potential implications, while Barbara is the other way around—starting with the human potential implications and moving toward the applications. And, of course, what she does is directly involved with both.

I was at Barbara's balcony, in Moscow, which looks like the place has been visited by a million birds. And it has! She puts food for birds there, and the birds even eat from her hands, and don't become nervous. She has a very close affinity for animals, and they respond to her. I met her cat—he's very, very nice. Some people used to say, "You own this cat? Is it *your* cat?" But I got the feeling from Barbara that she doesn't *own* a pet, they just *live together*. This is a very important sign to me, for if a person feels that the animal is living with them (and not that they *own* the pet), this tells me much about them and their attitudes. Such people feel a lot of respect for the animal and its needs, rather than just insisting that the animal be what they want it to be. So, this gave me a very special feeling for Barbara. She is extremely concerned about the well-being of animals in the Soviet Union and wants to do whatever possible to help people feel more warmly toward animals—even to the extent of simply giving them little pictures to stick on their wall! Her house is full of pictures of animals. Every place you look are pictures of animals or cartoons of animals—it's very funny! So there you are in Moscow, looking around at hundreds of animal pictures—dogs, cats, horses, and others. It's very unusual!

We met with some of Barbara's friends and students of the "Park Academy," which she also calls the "Star Club" (because they meet outside, near the Star cinema, and go to the park). Everything is very open, and anyone can come and see that there is nothing subversive or political in their activities, just the interest of people to better understand themselves as human beings. Barbara's friends are quite affirmative about her capabilities as a healer and about her teaching them different psi skills. I did not go deeply into this "evaluation," however, and, as a "scientist," what can I say, not having conducted any laboratory tests? But a human being who is in pain doesn't care whether it was checked out in a laboratory or not, he/she cares whether or not he/she can get help. But I didn't have a chance to check on this either, although I believe there are some people who really did get help from Barbara.

I got the feeling that Barbara is a very straightforward person; I did not get the feeling that she was doing anything special for me. I clearly felt that she was very committed to what she was doing, and that's a big difference. I see her interest in healing as part of her general empathy for people and other forms of life in general. She does not have to be feeding birds on her balcony in Moscow, so why does she do that? Because she has a feeling for life. I think that it is this feeling which keeps her alive through very difficult times. With all her problems, she still maintains her sense of humor; you see her laughing and smiling and joking. This to me is a sign of a healthy person—she can laugh about her troubles.

Barbara is a very strong person. Despite her own problems, she did not ask anything for herself, she only asked for things that would help in her work (writing, lecturing, researching) and also things (pictures, stickers, cards, articles) which would help to educate people about animals—to love animals. This was most striking for me. I think that if they were taking Barbara off to the electric chair, and on the way she saw a mouse in pain, she would stop to try to do something for the mouse, "Just a minute, excuse me, we have time, don't we?" And if she were sick and going to the hospital, she would probably stop and help some other living creature.

It is extremely important for Barbara to be able to write her ideas down and to communicate. Having a pen or pencil and a piece of paper is very important for her, and batteries for her tape recorder, too—so that she can speak her ideas and write papers. A pen and a piece of paper or a magnetic tape is her link with the outside world. And I think this is also what keeps her going—her feeling for people and for animals, and being able to write and communicate.

I think having her ideas in a book is a major thing for her. Barbara is an explorer. She and others like her will be explorers no matter where they live. She is part of a larger community of people around the world who don't know each other and have never met, but we are part of the same group of people who care about extending the capabilities of human beings.

A human being is part of the whole, called by us "Universe," a part limited in time and space. He experiences himself, his thoughts and feelings, as something separated from the rest, a kind of optical delusion of his consciousness. This delusion is a kind of prison for us, restricting us to our personal desires and to affection for a few persons nearest to us. Our task must be to free ourselves from this prison by widening our circle of compassion to embrace all living creatures and the whole of nature in its beauty.

Albert Einstein

Barbara Ivanova sees herself as one who is favored with a special kind of dream, a person blessed with an important task and goal to fulfill in life. In whatever ways are available to her, she keeps the spirit of the true dreamer alive. She heals the physically and emotionally sick. She awakens in others the moral obligation to care for and love one another.... And when she says in her article that "you know you are on the right path because you experience gratitude, joy, deep feelings of happiness," you believe her.... She is jovial and optimistic. She says that she grows stronger as the challenge to continue her work grows more overwhelming. She is a warm and vibrant moral voice opening her heart to others in the bitterly cold streets and parks...of Moscow.

Dr. Thomas Dale Cowan
Editor, *Dream Network Bulletin*
Brooklyn, New York

■ VI.

"Everything for the Others"

If I am not for myself, who will be for me? But if I am only for myself, what am I? And if not now, when?

Rabbi Hillel

Warning for Parapsychologists and Psychics

Barbara Ivanova

In this brief selection, Barbara discusses precautionary measures for students and researchers of psi phenomena. Her experience as a student and teacher of psi enables her to arrive at concrete suggestions and guidance for a grounded and healthy approach to psi. — Eds.

■ As I have mentioned a number of times, I believe that everyone possesses psi abilities to different degrees, and everyone can train and develop them to noticeably improve psi performance. However, there have been some cases when psi experiments and training (especially in the fields of psychokinesis and psychic healing) have led to temporary negative effects. In the process of our work devoted to the study and prevention of negative reactions and sensations which may be "by-products" of psi exercises, experiments, training, etc., we have found that negative reactions occur when certain rules and precautions, as well as psycho-hygiene and protection of the psychic's health, are not observed. These negative reactions are as follows:

1. *Tingling*: strong to more or lesser degrees, on the face, hands, feet, and all over the body. This is often connected with a feeling of warmth or heat, sometimes exceedingly tormenting.

2. *Muscular contractions*: sometimes very strong.

3. *Giddiness*: sometimes with complete loss of consciousness.

4. *Perspiration*: more or less profuse.

5. *Exhaustion*: utter weakness and depletion as consequences of psi activities (clairvoyance, PK, healing, etc.), if they are practiced for a longer period of time than the energy of the psychic or his/her skill are affording.

6. *Feeling of fever*: shivering, coldness, weakness, as a consequence of energy loss on a great scale.

7. *Loss of weight*: sometimes 800–1,000 grams after thirty minutes of work.

8. *High concentration of sugar in the blood*: up to the level which occurs in diabetes.

9. *Blood-pressure changes*: sometimes to a dangerous extent.

10. *Stress-like brainwaves*: EEG's chart as when under strong emotional excitement.

11. *Heart dysfunctions*: pulse beats faster or almost imperceptibly, electrocardiograms have indicated arhythmical heart activity.

12. *Loss of coordination*: on rare occasions.

13. *Temporary loss of taste, smell or other senses*: they can alter or deviate from reality—sometimes non-existent sensations or over-sensibility appear.

14. *Disturbance of endocrine system functioning*: on rare occasions.

15. *Pains*: in legs, hands and other parts of the body.

16. *Respiration disorder*: profuse, or exceedingly small.

17. *Loss or disturbance of sleep*: occurs frequently.

18. *General depression*: irritability or other signs of exhaustion of the nervous system, as well as many other symptoms of malfunction.[*]

All of these disorders can be felt for minutes, hours or days, and some of them even for months, if necessary measures are not taken. The disorders have been confirmed by objective methods of medical examination and by observation of the conditions of the psychic, as well as subjectively, through statements from the psychics. We can view these disorders as a stress-response, in varying degrees, by the organism. This supports the idea of the real nature of the phenomena which find physical means for their expression. The bioenergy of the body plays an important part in the process, and we must take care not to exhaust it, but to be careful with psychics, to spare their physical and mental health.

We can avoid these negative responses of mind and body by gradually training the psychic and exposing the body to the influence of our psi energies or that of other psychics only to a degree compatible with the psychic's potential. For instance, we start exercises once a week or once a ten-day period (as I did when I felt exhausted and experienced some of the symptoms described while

---

[*] It is worthwhile to mention also the cases when a nonexperienced healer is reported to attract a patient's disease to himself, i.e., he feels the same condition which he is striving to alleviate so as to help his patient. To prevent such cases a healer should observe rules of psycho-hygiene (e.g., regime, diet, ethical standards, etc.). Some healers also suggest that a student of healing should learn specific techniques of "protection."—Eds.

training clairvoyance and other qualities. This was in 1973, when I started the first training group and had not yet gained experience.)

In our group we discovered that it is better to work no more than fifteen to twenty minutes at one time, with breaks longer than the duration of the experiments. If the psychic copes well with training on this agenda, he can continue to work more frequently and for longer periods. If one does not feel well, working periods should be shortened. And beware: if psi energy is overused, the psychic can become disturbed and even ill. We have observed such cases.

It is important to be aware of the fact that it is not the psi-practicing itself which can harm the psychic or his subject, but only psi "illiteracy." This illiteracy—the lack of real knowledge or information as well as serious study in the field of psi phenomena—is truly dangerous in this work. Even more dangerous is the new form of superstition which merely denies all facts of psi phenomena, depriving people of the possibility of using their faculties in the right way. We cannot stop gifted psychics from becoming clairvoyant or receiving "information-PK" messages, so it is better if they understand the processes and know the rules for conducting these kinds of activities.

Negative attitudes of people about their gifts may also have a disastrous effect: psychics try to conceal these abilities, become frightened, or consider themselves mental cases. It creates a serious social problem: such people sometimes become uncommunicative or mentally ill because they feel it necessary to suppress these natural, inherent qualities. Or, they begin exploiting their abilities on a large scale without proper instruction, which may result in disaster. It is preferable that psychics understand the phenomena fundamental to their abilities, otherwise they can become extremely frightened when involuntarily producing psi-effects. With a negative background, traditions, social surroundings, and no one in whom to confide or get advice, the psychic may suffer not only mentally, but also physically.

If a person has psi-faculties (and a great percentage of people have them to a large degree without being aware of it), these should *not* be suppressed, or the individual could suffer from stress. Use should occur under the guidance of experienced persons, good books, in proper surroundings, and *with the right goals*. One should never try to get or to give psi information for personal gain, or which could harm others or to reveal others' secrets. Don't forget the "Law of Boomerang"—it will hit you when you least expect it! The same is true for healing: who are we to challenge the principles of karma? We cannot do it!

All these are well known things, but there are many people who are unaware of them. So this brief section will remind you of these rules. I hope it will help the beginners, experimenters, and psychics to master the art and science of parapsychology. Our experience, briefly presented here, might be useful for psychics, their parents, friends, teachers, and physicians to advance their work and to acquire the right attitude.

Meaningful Messages in Dreams

Barbara Ivanova

In considering psi information in dreams, Barbara again uses parapsy-chological principles as a means to express her belief in "One for all, All for one." Her strong spiritual basis is revealed for the reader as she urges us to listen, respect and follow our own inner guidance.—Eds.

■ Many people know that we are getting guidance from dreams, yet we seldom use it properly. We do not think enough about it, and do not analyze, nor pay enough attention to this very impor-tant part of our life. And there is often a key or information about how to behave or what to expect, which could positively change our life—if understood as it should be. Sometimes it is in symbols, other times it comes directly, or almost directly, in pictures, or even words of counsel and help. Everyone receives such information in his own code, which depends on many factors. For example, for Russians, the birch is a symbol of their homeland, but for Brazilians it is the palm. A Brazilian living in Europe who dreams of a palm could feel that it was time to go home.

But not only specific scenes and objects are important. We can distinguish a meaningful dream from an unimportant one by its very high emotional coloring. We do not forget it for a long time—even if we understood its meaning immediately. It remains deep in our thoughts and memory. Also, people generally receive their meaningful dreams in color rather than black and white. Even people who usually dream only in black and white will get their meaningful dreams in normal life-coloring, sometimes in very bright, unusually brilliant colors. Poor coloring in dreams may signify a poor emotional life, poor personal development of the individual, a low moral level, scant interest in the fate of others, or egotistic goals. Exceptions depend upon the level of dream-guidance and other factors.

Here are some examples of clear picture-symbols in meaningful dreams which show the way of life, the situation, or the action which must be undertaken in certain circumstances.

1. The dreamer is in a small boat, in rough seas during a storm. The water is dark, the sky menacing, and the boat is rolling and rocking dangerously. Disaster is imminent. There are some friends in the boat, all fighting with the storm. But some time later the weather clears, the sea becomes calmer and calmer, the sun appears, and all are safe. This dream was an answer to the inner question of the dreamer: *What will happen to us and our struggle in the present circumstances?*

2. The next dream was an answer to the inner question: *What should I do?* The dreamer sees that he is climbing a very steep rock, covered with ice and snow. The wind is stormy and tears him from the rock, leaving his fingers bleeding and nails broken because of his attempts to hold with bare hands to the icy rocks. It is dark and very cold. He is tired and frightened, but again he climbs and climbs. Then he feels that he cannot endure longer and wants to return. He looks down—but as he looks, he feels the absolute impossibility of returning into the dark abyss. It is much more dangerous. So he makes his final effort—and finds himself on a very small plateau, where he can rest a little. But he knows that his only way is up the rock. The sun appears above him and the summit is clear and golden. Once again he begins his effort to reach the peak, rested and knowing that he has no other way, only up, to the light, at any cost!

3. Another very significant dream followed the inner question: *Why must I suffer the ordeals of a hopeless fight, which is dangerous, incommensurate with my resources, and seemingly endless?* In the dream, he saw himself on the side of a long road, covered with sunshine. From across the road a large crowd arrives, led by a clergyman in white garments. There is a shining banner in front of the crowd, with a simple white cross on it. The dreamer feels that he, too, should walk with the crowd. Then he hears, in French, the following words: *Tout pour les autres* (Everything for the others). He understood that he must give all his life for the others and go with them, following the white cross of spirituality, on life's sunny road.

4. The following dream has a very deep meaning, with a clear message. The dreamer is in a dark, swampy forest, at night, and has lost his way. He is in a desperate state, not knowing where to go and wallowing in the morass. He is not religious, but he falls on his knees and begins to pray, imploring the Higher Forces to help him out of the forest and to show him the way. Suddenly a clear

ray of light appears from the black sky, moving and showing a stable way among the bog. He rushes forward. But after some steps he loses his way and again feels very frightened and lonely. He falls on his knees again, praying and begging for guidance and help. And the golden ray reappears from above, leading him out of the dark, swampy, dangerous forest. He goes astray three or four times and loses his way, but after every sincere and deep prayer the helpful golden beam always reappears to show him the right direction out of the darkness and bog. A very clear indication indeed! His prayer was right: he asked no favors or gifts, only the right way.

Individuals who are gifted with this kind of dream have an important task and goal to fulfill in life. If one goes the right way, all is well. The main principle is to understand, to follow, and to respect the guidance (which everyone obtains in different ways). It is important not to misuse these channels or prayers for petty or egotistic goals.

Many people know now that we are receiving help and counsel constantly, and not only in dreams. We may get sudden impulses: not to go this or that way, to do or not to do certain things, to undertake travels or not, etc. We are happy when we learn to distinguish the real "hints," the true guiding impulses, from fear, laziness, pride, and other false, misleading feelings. It is important not only for us in our personal lives, but for others, whom we could (and must) help on our way. Thus we fulfill the primary task in our existence, learning to see, to distinguish clearly, to follow the important guidance which we are constantly receiving.

But here is another very important side of our problem: how do we distinguish the real messages we receive from the Higher Realms from false and low guidance? It is not so difficult as it seems to be since the right messages are connected and accompanied with feelings of gratitude, happiness, joy, and deep, positive emotions. They appear in an atmosphere of a profound sense of duty, bliss and absolute truth. No low feelings are involved, no base interests. And if we follow their guidance, our life changes dramatically for the best. And, what is more important, for the best of all those surrounding us. We are more and more happy, in all circumstances!

155

From the "Winged Elephant" — to the "Winged Horse"

Barbara Ivanova

With this final selection by Barbara Ivanova, we find her again building bridges between people and realities. Basing her discussion on a recent Japanese book concerning the chakras, Barbara finds harmony between East and West. She urges further collaboration between Western empiricism and Eastern mysticism (which is understood as an intuitive way of acquiring knowledge and understanding of human nature and the Universe) in order that the slowly prodding elephant of skeptical Western science may evolve into a modern flying Pegasus that suitably honors the human spirit and its potential.—Eds.

■ For many decades established science was too pragmatic to understand the roots and causes, the inner meaning and the real connections between investigated facts and natural phenomena—the way they lead our thoughts and influence our lives. Recent years have seen a new breakthrough, however, which helps us to overcome the limits of statistics and "digital thought" (our superficial "finger-philosophy"—that is, the ruling idea that the only things real and true are those we can touch with the "fingers" of formal control methods). Now the time is ripe to give more attention to the truth: the inner realities, the main instrument of connection with the Universe—the human being. One of the merits of such books as the *Theories of the Chakras: Bridge to Higher Consciousness* by Dr. Hiroshi Motoyama (Japan, 1981) is exactly this line of investigation of these connections. His studies are a true bridge between the empirical dimension of today's science, and the inner dimensions of Higher Awareness. Works on this level help us to draw deeper conclusions from all our superficial knowledge of this tragic, transitional age.

Science touches the ground of simple physical laws with all its "feet" and weight. And this is as it should be. But science cannot exist without the wings of free and daring thought, without a broad understanding of events and their deep meaning, without the moral and ethical teachings and conclusions needed by Man so much. The times when naked facts predominated—without their inner values, without the teachings which they give us, without their educational meaning—are over now. We grew out of them. The heavy "elephant" of the accepted, admitted science has strong legs—but has weak wings of thought. Without this sufficient inner elevation he cannot support his clumsy body. Today the scientific elephant is a lesser impedance to the real evolution of Man. The ancient tale about a winged horse, which could be accepted as a poetic image of humanity's future development, shows us the real way: hooves on the ground—but with a slim body and mighty wings, elevating us to the sky!

The winged horse will overcome the inflexible, heavy "elephant" of yesterday's notions, which has impeded the development of our knowledge in the realms of the Universal Laws. In terms of scientific investigation, we must connect the results of our experiments, supported by modern technology (the "hooves") with the "wings" of ancient knowledge, moral teachings, and ethical conclusions—as Dr. Motoyama did in his book.

It is right, as Motoyama notes, that the highest teachings can be taught only to earnest, well prepared disciples. Many dangers can arise if we give them to morally low, unstable, or immature persons. We have seen it often in our own work, when individuals use their new siddhis to master self-affirmation, material enrichment, and even worse goals. It is easy to buy and persuade such people, and they violate the Cosmic Laws. This is the main reason why we do not teach healing, clairvoyance, etc., as we did before—to any person who wanted it. Today only selected individuals have the right to such knowledge, for it is a double-edged tool.

Europe has much to learn from ancient Eastern wisdom. This bridge, which our civilization needs, is created by scientists and priests—and Dr. Motoyama plays both roles. Knowledge cannot be separated from ethical ways of education, or we have tragedies, of which there are many examples in human history. East and West must melt together and learn to understand each other.

Of importance are the recommendations by Dr. Leadbeater cited in the book by Dr. Motoyama. First of all, we have "to devote time and energy to the betterment of society before indulging in practices designed to awaken kundalini." This is rarely stressed in other books—and therefore many practitioners go a dangerous way, led by egotism, false pride, separation from the needs and fates of others (even harming them purposely), etc. Such individuals were not first taught (and are unable to understand) that the main task is not their own yoga training to attain certain skills and powers, but to help others, and in their purification to clear the way for others and clean the karma of the whole world.

Sri Aurobindo, one of the greatest teachers, said it this way: We must participate in the life of the society, to help the good cause, and not to limit our work and life only to self-development. What would this be for? (But logically, of course, we must first understand what is truth and the good cause.)

It is premature to give the weapon of High Knowledge to unawakened, narrow-minded persons of low moral and ethical level. It is even dangerous for society. The same occurs with the development of simple psi faculties. We have clearly seen this in the results of our training and lecturing activities: those students who do not follow our advice and allow themselves to be attracted to negative ways of using their para-skills (according to their low mentality and life-purposes) find disaster, not only for them personally (the well known Law of Boomerang), but for those around them.

Motoyama's book states, "The paranormal abilities which result from the awakening of the svadhisthana—telepathy, clairvoyance, clairaudience, etc.—may not be entirely free of self-interest, negativity, personal emotion and other undesirable mental attributes." But, "the siddhis, realized when the manipura awakens, are of a benevolent and compassionate nature." Only such persons have the moral right to use their para-faculties. On this level they can help the society—and not endanger it with their para-powers. Teachers and gurus must be very careful in choosing their chelas or disciples. This is the first thing which we as parapsychologists have to consider—and we must act accordingly in our work. We are grateful to Dr. Motoyama for these warnings.

There are very significant indications in the book about the three major categories of karmic debt: "(a) that accruing from an individual's past incarnations; (b) that inherited from his family; and (c) that resulting from actions of his society or social group. All these factors contribute to an individual's karma; they must be dealt with. It is impossible to avoid one's karma."

From this statement we are compelled to derive very important conclusions: the individual is responsible for the society! Otherwise he would not have to bear the consequences of society's actions, direction, manner, etc.—on his own karma. It is one of the expressions of the "collective karma," which we all forge together for ourselves. If this was known in the world more widely, perhaps the fate of many nations would be different than what it is now. No one has the right to sit in an "ivory tower," letting others do anything they want with his society. We find that true yoga supports not egotistical conduct, not weakness of heart and mind (under the cover of high words, or under any disguise and excuses), not camouflaged cowardice—but right conduct, active position, a sense of responsibility and civil courage.

We must understand—and act accordingly—that everyone must participate in the life of society, in a just, humane degree and direction, and not withdraw oneself from it and try to throw the responsibility on others. Everyone is responsible—whether we admit it or not. The result of passivity or negative attitudes will be unavoidable tragic karma. It is one of the Universal Laws. Everyone has to be conscious of it and to teach others. We are very grateful to Dr. Motoyama for these clear teachings!

Another point of Dr. Motoyama's is also very important to understand, "Such negative conditions as poverty, disease, emotional conflict, etc., should be considered ultimately beneficial occurrences." As a teacher and educator by profession, and with thirty years experience in instruction, I am interested first of all in questions of education. Such questions are insufficiently explained in other books. We must draw our conclusions out of adversities and difficulties, and must learn to value them as our teachers and advisers, our school of life.

Nicolaus Roerich said, too, "One sees that the West and East are working together on many principles." We see it now even more clearly, as in his time, he foresaw it. The splendid book by Dr. Motoyama is one of the signs that this is true.

Let us hope that the mighty wings of ancient Eastern thought will be able to elevate the clumsy "elephant" of Western science to an awareness of the essence and real purport of what the scientists are doing with their devices, numbers and statistics. Let us hope that the majority of modern scientists will be able to draw the necessary, inevitable conclusions (of which they are still afraid, qualifying them as "unscientific"), and finally to grasp the inner reality of things which have been so clear in Eastern thought for thousands and thousands of years. Let us hope that books like the work of Nicolaus Roerich, Dr. Motoyama, and other thinkers help us to convert the "winged elephant" of yesterday's science into the famous winged horse, which is able to stand on his feet—and to fly in the sky, towards the new realms of our future knowledge. And let us hope that this book, as a bridge to Higher Consciousness, leads the readers to the light and joy of real understanding: knowing our place among other creatures, our goal in life, our task in the Universe.

I would like to conclude in agreement with the last words of Dr. Motoyama's book: "I feel that the continuation of research into the nature of psi energies, by many others as well as myself, will lead to considerable change in our views of matter, of mind and body, of human beings, and of the world itself."

In Lieu of a Conclusion:
Ascending the Blue Mountain

Larissa Vilenskaya

■ With tears in my eyes I read Maria's account of her trip to the Soviet Union and her meeting with Barbara. Here she is, an American woman, kind, sympathizing, willing to help, to become an intermediary between us, two halves of the whole divided by the ruthless border between the two countries. My messenger, my envoy, my hope. Frankly speaking, at first I did not have much hope. It takes years and years of living in a society like the Soviet Union to understand its nature, its peculiarities, and the everyday life of ordinary people there. And without this understanding it is almost impossible to comprehend Barbara's situation, her problems, her difficulties.

However, Barbara and I were lucky to find such a friend. I understood this clearly while reading Maria's account. Everything went vividly before my eyes as if I was there yesterday: this cozy one-room apartment (not one bedroom, but just one room and a small kitchen), flowers on the balcony, and the funny cat Yashka. Barbara and I lived together for about two years, have been friends and colleagues for almost fifteen years, and have been separated "in space" for more than six years. Having said farewell words to each other at Moscow's Sheremet'yevo airport, I left her for an indefinite period of time. After three years of waiting for my exit visa, I was fortunate enough to leave for Israel and later to come to the United States. My long-awaited exit visa said "for permanent residence." That is, for good, forever. An emigrant from the Soviet Union has no right to visit his/her friends and relatives. And, therefore, ours was an indefinite separation.

Mail, as slow as a snail and as unreliable as a thief, was the only link between us—mail, plus this unknown kind of communication which we call telepathy, ESP, or psi. Through the years of this separation, I have always felt when Barbara was not well, when she had troubles, when she was thinking about me. And now,

Maria's trip, this miracle. Looking at Barbara's photographs, I virtually heard her deep voice saying, "...but the rooster doesn't know!" These are words from a joke, one of numerous jokes she knows and likes to use at the "appropriate" time. The joke is as follows:

A madman believes that he is a barley seed and that a rooster will eat him. He is taken to a mental hospital, where an experienced psychiatrist works with him for a long time, using all the available powers of contemporary medical science. Finally, the doctor decides that his patient has recovered and can be discharged from the hospital. He invites the patient into his office and tells him, "You have completely recovered now. You know that you are not a barley seed, you are a human being."

"Yes, I know that I am a human being," the patient nods. They go together into the street, and the psychiatrist is ready to say "good bye" to his patient. Suddenly the patient notices a rooster and runs away as fast as he can.

"Why?" the psychiatrist asks surprisingly. "Now you know that you are not a seed, you are a human being."

"Yes, I know," the patient answers, "but the **rooster** doesn't know!"

Barbara and I often mentioned this joke. "The rooster doesn't know" refers to the Soviet authorities who forbid virtually all unauthorized (even non-political) groups and gatherings. Although our interest was the potential of the human mind and the mysteries of human nature, and we were not engaged in any kind of political activity, we were continually treated as "seeds" and obstacles to our work always appeared. Our activities were of a solely scientific character but "the rooster didn't know!"

In my opinion, this is a major reason why, despite her outstanding research results, Barbara encountered many obstacles to her work. In 1973 she was unexpectedly fired from her job as a Portuguese language instructor at the Moscow State Institute for International Relations, where she had been employed for twenty-six years.

This sad story began on October 31, 1973, when a certain Goncharov, temporarily functioning as Staff Director of the Institute, informed her that either she must write a statement of "resignation at her own volition," or she would be fired on the basis of having "indulged in charlatanry and given lectures incompatible with the calling of a teacher." At issue were her scientific lectures on healing and other parapsychological topics. Through blackmail and threats, she was forced to write such a statement and was dismissed in violation of Soviet labor laws.

She appealed to the court, requesting reinstatement of her position. The court, however, instead of punishing the lawbreakers (who dismissed her), supported them, and in so doing violated existing legislation. But this was only the beginning of her troubles. The unwarranted closing of the Laboratory for Bioinformation deprived Barbara of a place to conduct her research work, or to teach healing and other psi qualities. In order to gather with a group of her students and followers, she literally found herself on the sidewalk. Since then, her group (called the "Park Academy" or "Star Club") meets all year under open skies.

The entire extent of ridicule heaped on her by the authorities cannot be fully detailed here: her lectures were disrupted, provocations made against her, and she was continually threatened by imprisonment and incarceration in a psychiatric hospital. She has been unemployed since 1973. It is very difficult to understand the reasons for such treatment of a researcher who carries out very useful and necessary activities, returning people to health and enhancing their creative potential and capacity to work.

In 1975 the Bioinformation Laboratory was closed down. A new Bioelectronics Laboratory was established in Moscow in place of the closed lab in 1978, and was directed by Alexander Spirkin, a well-known Soviet philosopher and an Associate Member of the USSR Academy of Sciences. He organized a research group at the new lab, which included many physicians, in order to explore issues of psychic healing. However, officially appointed members of the Board of Directors of the Bioelectronics Laboratory imposed such tight restrictions upon its participants that researchers like Barbara would never agree to work there, preferring to meet with colleagues in the "Park Academy" or "Star Club" in any weather.

Barbara takes all these troubles with profound understanding, as a climber on the mountain described in one of her "meaningful dreams." She believes that life is a school and ordeals are to test us, to educate, to make one stronger and more human, to teach sympathy and understanding. Therefore, we must be happy to encounter difficulties and to be able to overcome them. Writing about a guidance-dream, she clearly described her perception of the situation:

As the dreamer, Barbara was between a dark, cold valley and a high mountain, shining in the sun. She thought, "I must go down to the poor people who live in that dark valley—but I will go later. Now my task is to climb this steep, snowy mountain." She began the ascent. Moving quickly and energetically like a flying bird, she was in a strong, certain, and very happy state of mind.

On the way up she encountered a stout man, with a kind smile, who said, "What are you doing? It is very dangerous to climb the mountain in this speed and manner. Be more careful!"

Her dreamer answered, "Yes, I know! Thank you! But I am so happy in doing so!" And so she proceeded in her gay, rapid, birdlike ascent, ever higher and higher! And always, she knows she will return to the valley to help those left in the dark.

Believing in the meaning and necessity of her work, and listening to her inner guidance, all day, every day, Barbara continues to work on what she feels is of paramount importance: to help people untap their powers, and to attain a higher spiritual level and understanding of their destiny in the world and universe.

One thing Barbara cannot do: she cannot be indifferent. If a pet, an animal, or a person is in trouble, she immediately runs to help, without a second thought whether it would be difficult or even dangerous for her to provide this help. While being with her in a number of such situations, I often recalled the words of the writer, Bruno Yasensky. *"Don't be afraid of your enemies,"* he wrote, *"the worst they can do is to kill you. Don't be afraid of your friends: the worst they can do is to betray you. But do be afraid of those who are indifferent: they don't kill and they don't betray, but it is with their knowledge and consent that betrayal and murder exist in the world."* And I am still extremely grateful to you, Barbara, for reminding me of this rule of life.

Soon after coming to Israel and struggling in my attempts to start a new life, I received a New Year's greeting from Barbara with excerpts from a book in English which included:

belie that life with all its complications and hardships is worth living.

belie that I can give love, accept love and share love.

belie that life is what I make it, that I am *master* of *my fate*.

I know, Barbara, that you have been following these principles yourself and I am very grateful to you once again for this reminder.

I hope that Barbara's writings will be appreciated and she will be given opportunities to continue her research and activities. The recent arousal of interest in healing in the USSR and numerous publications on the subject by the national press support such a hope. While thinking about Barbara's situation, I often remember a wise Brazilian fairy tale which Barbara once translated from Portuguese into Russian. Translating it now into English, I believe that it is not too distorted after two translations.

"Once upon a time, poor people were living in a far away, strange land. One morning a citizen of this country woke up and suddenly saw a blue mountain far away—a beautiful, brilliant mountain. He began to show it to others—the mountain was so magnificent, so beautiful. He wanted everyone to enjoy seeing it! But the others did not see anything. And the person who saw the blue mountain was killed, for it was the law of this unfortunate land that they killed those who saw things which others did not see.

Many years passed by, and one day an individual, who was involved in the death of the first person, suddenly saw a magnificent blue mountain shining before his very eyes. It was amazing and beautiful, as if inviting him to climb it. 'Isn't this a dream?' He did not believe himself. 'Is it true that the blue mountain exists in reality? Does this mean that the individual who was killed spoke the truth?' He began to tell others about his discovery, yet no one saw the blue mountain. And he also was killed, in the same way as the man who was the first to see the beautiful mountain.

After many years other people appeared who were able to see the high, proud, and illuminating mountain. There were more and more such people. However, all of them were killed—for most of the people of this land still did not see anything.

Years and years passed by. The unfortunate people of this land experienced many troubles, wars, and disasters. And their eyes, washed with tears from suffering, were able to see the mysterious blue mountain. Now, when everyone saw this blue miracle, they felt it impossible that they could not see it previously. And they could not understand how it happened that they killed the best people of their land."

I believe that a happy ending happens not only in fairy tales but sometimes also in real life. I believe that our separation from Barbara is not forever. I very much appreciate, Maria, what you have done for both of us. And this book is our present to you, dear Barbara, in the hope that we will be fortunate enough to see each other again "in this lifetime."

A Few Additional Words— My Story

Larissa Vilenskaya

■ *The Golden Chalice* had been completed almost a year ago when Maria Mir and I initiated our attempts to find a publisher. Now, that the H. S. Dakin company has agreed to publish the book, this is in the past. Yet, rereading my notes in preparation of the final version of the manuscript, I realized that my attempt to write about Barbara and about our work and friendship is incomplete without writing more about my own path. Usually, it is difficult for me to write about myself, but unexpectedly, these pages have been completed quickly—within several hours of non-stop (almost obsessive) work. Although I have used some of my earlier notes, other passages came instantaneously, virtually in a ready form, as though through automatic writing—without thinking, assessing, rewriting, or correcting.

I was born in Riga, Latvia, after it was a part of Russia or, more exactly, the Soviet Union. I finished high school in a Ukrainian town, Poltava. In high school I was a bit of an odd-ball—the other girls with their interests in boys, fashionable clothes and dancing seemed to me very superficial and often boring. Instead, I was deeply interested in unusual, extraordinary phenomena, especially those associated with the human mind. Rather than going to a party, I preferred to sit somewhere in a corner with an obscure book found in the local library. With great interest I made my way through the quite technical work of engineer Bernard Kazhinsky, *Biological Radio Communication*; a more popular text by Leonid Vasiliev (Professor of Physiology at Leningrad University), *Mysterious Phenomena of the Human Psyche*; and later, during my first year in an engineering college in Moscow, I found Vasiliev's major scientific publication, *Experimental Studies in Mental Suggestion*.

During my first year of college, an unexpected event happened that became the first in a long chain of events which completely changed my life. Or was it not unexpected, but meant to be?...

Was it my destiny? My karma? A prelude to my mission in this world? And do I have one? Does everyone have one? I didn't have answers to those questions then, and I haven't found them now .... But let me return to this event.

In 1967 I witnessed a lecture-demonstration by Karl Nikolayev and Yuri Kamensky, the well-known telepathic team, with whom Soviet scientists have been working for some time. The test was made in two different rooms. It was an ESP test, in which Kamensky was given an object to send to Nikolayev telepathically. It was a sort of metal chain or necklace. But a friend of mine had an interesting idea: maybe we could interfere with the session and send our own image. The idea was to understand whether this was a stage performance, magic tricks, or whether we were really seeing the interaction of human minds.

Nikolayev was isolated in a distant room and my friend and I decided to concentrate on sending him the image of a magnet. For several minutes we concentrated on a magnet I had brought by chance from the physics lab. I imagined Nikolayev standing behind me and looking at the magnet over my shoulder. Of course we had no way of knowing what the psychic was reporting; the results of the experiment were known only after the demonstration had been concluded.

Everything Nikolayev said in the other room was transcribed. Afterward we found out that he began by describing the necklace —long, thin, metal, and golden-colored—but then he began to describe our magnet as rectangular, metal, gray-silver, its approximate size and so on. Later, he went back to the necklace. This proved to us that we could interfere with a telepathy experiment and make a successful telepathic transmission.

This event led me to serious interest in psi phenomena and parapsychology. I came to the Laboratory for Bioinformation of the A.S. Popov Scientific and Technological Society for Radio Engineering and Communication in Moscow, first as a volunteer and later as the head of the lab's Experimental and Training Group. Soon I was fortunate enough to work with Rosa Kuleshova, who specialized in "fingertip vision" or "eyeless sight." It was fascinating to observe Rosa identifying colors with her fingers even when the samples were placed under several layers of opaque paper, and I myself did not know the colors. But even more fascinating was to know that Rosa had learned this ability through persistent exercises while working with the blind. I began toying with the idea that I could develop similar powers, and from the very beginning of my attempts to study these extraordinary qualities, I came to the conclusion that researchers of psi phenomena should not only study these abilities in others, but try to develop them in themselves.

I tried, and although I can't say I learned to read with my fingers, I was successful at identifying colors, large letters and drawings. Soon I started training others in this kind of dermo-optic perception. While most of the girls in my group eventually learned some degree of "skin vision," another outcome of the project was more interesting.

This began in 1969, shortly before working with Rosa Kuleshova, when I became a student of a psychic healer, Sergei Vronsky, who was also working at the Laboratory for Bioinformation. I was twenty-one at that time, very shy and unsure of myself. Vronsky assured me that he could see whether people had the ability to heal and that I could do healing through the laying-on of hands if I committed myself to learning and sympathizing with another individual's suffering. He taught us various visualization techniques and directed us to concentrate on a sense of energy flowing through our hands.

"If the patient suffers from a headache," Vronsky coached his students, "you may imagine the headache as a fog and relieve the patient of it by thinking of dispersing the fog and using the energy of your hands to achieve this." I first attempted to use this technique to relieve a girlfriend's headache. The girl was sitting with her eyes closed, and when I "saw" in my mental picture that all the fog was dispersed, the girl opened her eyes and, to my amazement, asked, "What have you done? It's gone!" Later I came intuitively to the idea of color healing, without knowing about numerous Western publications and practitioners advocating this method. This happened after my first attempts at skin vision, when we discovered that the development of dermo-optic perception enhances the individual's sensitivity to the human biological field (the aura) and the capacity to perceive colors, the structure of the aura and to make a diagnosis.

I began working with several persons who had previously learned skin vision and discovered that many of them felt a slight prickly feeling (tingling and/or vibration) while moving their hands along a human body, some five to fifteen inches from it. This, we believed, was produced by an interaction between the person's

169

hand and the human biofield (aura). We learned that a person with no complaints has a biofield which is more or less regular—even or predictable. But when the patient had some disorder, my students and I felt a distortion (disequilibrium) in the energy field. Most often we could not explain it in medical terms for all of us had little medical knowledge. At that time I began to give talks about psychic phenomena and healing.

When the talk was for a non-medical audience I usually avoided demonstrations of diagnosis and healing, since I did not want to turn my presentation into something like a circus performance. But while lecturing for a medical audience, I often successfully demonstrated diagnosis by pointing out where the patients had problems —inflammations, tumors, ulcers, scars from previous operations, etc. Although I was interested in the possibilities which this kind of diagnosis seemed to open and I liked to be able to help people, I was more intrigued with a much broader possibility—to show people their hidden potential. I said to myself, "We are all clairvoyants, we are all healers, we just need to allow ourselves to see, to feel, to experience."

About this time, in the beginning of the 1970s, I started working with Barbara at the Laboratory for Bioinformation. Soon, she became my teacher and my dearest friend. Although she never viewed our relationship in teacher/student terms, her vast knowledge, her amazing intuition, and her inexhaustible optimism brought much light and happiness into my life. Barbara, who has helped hundreds of individuals from various cities and towns throughout the Soviet Union to untap their healing powers, repeatedly cautioned us to be very careful with this kind of training:

> If one has the ability to radiate bioenergy, it is not enough to give one the right to heal. First of all, harmonization of both patient and healer is necessary, and only afterward one may try to send the energy. There can be no lasting results without a certain ethical and moral development.

Thanks to Barbara's suggestions, I understood that it was dangerous to lead people in the development of their healing powers without simultaneous spiritual development, for the same energies might be used not only in a positive, but also in a negative direction. To lead people to spiritual development, however, was extremely difficult (if not impossible) in contemporary Russia, where ESP was called "bioinformation" and the aura—"biofield."

While I was still pursuing my interest in many aspects of psi and self-development, and continuing to give lectures on parapsychology and healing, I decided not to lead any more training groups. In my meditations, I first came to a feeling and then to the decision, that I should completely change my life and leave the Soviet Union.

It took me about three painful years to obtain my exit visa from the USSR. During these years, I went through many troubles, the stress was unbearable, and I had to intentionally decrease my sensitivity. When I ultimately managed to leave (first to Israel and then to the United States) and emerged alone in a completely unfamiliar world I felt totally exhausted, spent, and depleted— physically, mentally, and spiritually. It seemed to me that I was many years behind regarding the development of my own psychic powers—much was lost, I thought, in this struggle for freedom. Although I tried to perform occasional healings to help friends, I did not feel like attempting to go any further, either in research or in self-development. I even stopped my meditations. When in 1981 I moved to the United States, I soon started *Psi Research* journal, an international quarterly on parapsychology and human potential studies. At that time I felt that writing was the only activity left for me, but two years later I found that it was not so.

At the beginning of 1983, I received an intriguing article from the Soviet Union. Entitled "Know Yourself," the article described a Soviet enthusiast of self-exploration, Valery Avdeyev, who demonstrated firewalking by crossing, unharmed, a thirty foot long bonfire glowing with coals, by acting on his firm belief in the virtually unlimited hidden human potential. "As soon as we subject our organism to extreme conditions," he reasoned, "in addition to instinctive protective mechanisms, other specific and subconscious defense mechanisms will be activated." Avdeyev described not only his first successful attempt at firewalking, but another occasion in which he "could not bring himself to the proper state of mind" and was burned. "This second attempt taught me a great deal," he wrote. "I understood that the primary factor necessary for walking on coals was to enter a state of consciousness in which this seemed possible. One could learn not only to play the violin, to run the 100 meter dash, to swim the breast-stroke, but also to desensitize oneself to fire...."

Soon I had an opportunity to convince myself that he was right through my own experience. In the fall of 1983, I was invited to a "firewalking workshop" in Portland, Oregon, conducted by a spiritual teacher from California, Tolly Burkan, who learned this art from a student of a Tibetan. Although Tolly promised to teach anyone to firewalk safely in less than four hours, I came there not intending to do anything so crazy as "to walk on fire," but rather to write about the workshop for the *Psi Research* journal. But when I witnessed Tolly walking on the red-hot coals, and then others, including a twelve-year-old girl who followed him, I remembered Avdeyev and asked myself, "If he could walk on those coals, if Tolly can, if others can do it, why can't I? They have the same skin and tissue as mine!" I felt that it was completely okay for me to participate. The coals, glowing bright orange, looked inviting and friendly. Suddenly I understood that I *could* do it, I *would* do it—and off I went! The coals were hot, but not unbearable—just like walking on hot sand. I felt exhilarated: "I did it! I did!"

Now I was certain: yes, firewalking is definitely possible even for untrained individuals. At the same time, I've studied physics and I know that human tissue usually does not withstand temperatures higher than 60°C (140°F), and the temperature of the coals often exceeds 600°C (1,200–1,300°F). What forces and mechanisms, then, protect the skin from burns? I thoroughly reviewed the available literature. Stories of people walking through infernos without harm have come from India, Greece, Bulgaria, Sri Lanka, the South Pacific, Africa, Indonesia and Japan. In a two-year study of Greek firewalkers, Dr. Vittoria Manganas administered medical and psychiatric tests. She believes that the crucial component is a clear knowing that one will succeed: "Greek, Filipino, Islamic and Indian fire dancers use different kinds of religious faith to achieve the strength of absolute belief."

It seems to me that now I understand what is happening at Tolly Burkan's firewalking workshop. When people actually see someone doing something that seems impossible (e.g., walking on fire!), they experience an instantaneous shift in their belief system which makes it possible for them to "unlearn" their limitations and to instantaneously "reprogram" themselves. Similarly, when Rosa Kuleshova demonstrated her skin vision capacities and then asked others to recognize colors or drawings with their eyes closed, many were successful, since they had just witnessed another person performing the "impossible feat."

Previously I had demonstrated aura diagnosis and healing which led people to believe in "impossible" powers, now I understood that I possessed a much more important "tool"—to be able to show how to walk on fire. Eureka!—this was what I needed. I returned to Tolly Burkan and said to him, "I want to study with you. I want to know everything you know. I want to understand the art of firewalking and to be able to conduct such workshops."

In May 1984, I was invited to participate in a three-week study tour with Tolly Burkan and his wife Peggy to become a "firewalking instructor"—to learn to conduct firewalking workshops. In the course of this training, Tolly and Peggy led us not only through breathing exercises and an American Indian sweatlodge, but also through unusual tests. Because the specific topic of Tolly's seminars is overcoming fear and limitations through firewalking, we, eleven trainees (including three women) were invited to break through our own fears and limitations. Tasks proposed to us during these "three weeks beyond the limits" included spelunking in the largest Californian cavern (which started with lowering ourselves 200 feet down on a rope), parachute jumping, spending a night alone in the forest and similar "trials." These proved to be much more difficult for me than firewalking since some of these tasks required a certain degree of physical fitness, which I lacked, but still had to meet the challenge. In starting to rappel or jump out of a plane (I made two parachute jumps) I thought, "I'll be in the hands of God! I know that physically I am not ready to do something like this, but I *can* and I will!"

While our team traveled throughout the west coast of the U.S., I witnessed hundreds of "unprepared" people walking across beds of hot coals after three to four hour seminars with no injuries other than an occasional blister. I became interested in whether any differences could be found between those who blister and those who emerge from the firebed completely unharmed. My preliminary observations indicate that at least there are no obvious, easily detectable differences. The only tendency I could pinpoint was that those who walked more confidently (not necessarily faster, and often quite the opposite) got blisters more rarely. When I asked Peggy Burkan whether she had an "anti-blistering" technique, her answer was immediate, "Sometimes I get blisters, too. Most important, don't go onto the fire casually! When I started getting blisters, I had to upgrade my energy." Her answer reminded me of what I read some time ago about firewalking in Polynesia.

At the beginning of the century, Colonel Gudgeon wrote about a firewalking ceremony in Polynesia, in which four Europeans participated. He described that the local priest (called *tohunga* in the dialect) and his disciple came to the Europeans, and the disciple handed one of them a branch of the *Ti* plant (*Dracaena*) as the priest said to him, "I hand my *mana* (power) over to you; lead your friends across." Gudgeon, who walked on the red-hot stones unharmed, emphasized in his account, "A man must have *mana* to do it; if he has not, it will be too late when he is on the hot stone.... I can only tell you it is *mana*—*mana tangata* and *mana atua*."

Is this just one more belief that can be dismissed as easily as the notion of observing a specific diet for successful firewalking (which is known in Greece and other countries)? Or are we again encountering this concept of "life energy" known as prana, chi, or mana? After all, some researchers (e.g., Joseph Chilton Pearce and Andrew Weil) indicate a clear connection between firewalking and healing:

> I agree with the firewalkers of Greece that the *power that protects them from burns can also cure disease* (emphasis added). The mind holds the key to healing, and healing is as extraordinary as firewalking. It may also make use of some nervous pathways and mechanisms. (Dr. Andrew Weil, *Health and Healing*, Boston: Houghton Mifflin, 1983, p. 249.)

Yogis maintain that prana heals, and Chinese chi-gong masters attribute the same quality to chi energy. I tend to believe that firewalking workshops which usually include collective singing, *auming*, chanting and other kinds of group interaction lead to "focusing the energy" of the participants (if we speak in these terms), to creating a unified, synergistic group energy. Barbara conducts mass healing sessions in which she works with the whole group in a similar way that she does when healing a single patient. She believes that the "group energy field" is created during this process. Another healer from Moscow, Alexander Maisyuk, discusses similar ideas:

> All the actions in which human beings participate can be subdivided into individual and collective. "Collective" suggests three or more people. When it is only two, it's still a personal act. In primitive societies, it is assumed that a collective, "team" consciousness has a greater degree of power and influence. This is all based on a relatively well known statement that a thought is an action. This confronts one of the basic questions of philosophy, "What is an action?"

Does the concept or idea of an action correspond to the action itself?... If so, we can possibly explain the phenomena and visions that occur in team healing or team praying.

When I studied firewalking with Tolly and Peggy Burkan, I received one more interesting hint in the same direction. The last day of our training course they conducted a type of "graduation ceremony" for our group, which included an ancient American Indian ritual with feathers. While Tolly was putting sage on burning charcoal and praying, Peggy asked us to come up to her, one by one, and moved the ritual feathers around the person, whispering something which was barely audible to the rest of the group. When I came up to her, I did not have any preconceptions or expectations as to what was supposed to happen—in fact, I respected the ritual but did not expect anything special. However, standing with my eyes closed, as was required, I felt a tremendous surge of energy through my body—the intensity I've never before experienced in my life. And then I heard Peggy's words, *"Take the power!"*

I agree that this concept of *external* energy leads to the same question as that asked by Dr. Weil, "Why do firewalkers from Fiji to Greece think their powers come from deities and saints rather than from their own minds?" I believe that there is no contradiction between the two approaches: we are *interconnected* with each other and with external forces and energies, known and unknown, and what is believed to be the powers of *our* minds may result from this global interconnectedness.

Soon after my apprenticeship with the Burkans, I started my own firewalking workshops in the United States and in Europe. Now I felt much more confident: I wanted to use firewalking as a tool, as a metaphor to lead people to overcoming fears and limiting beliefs, to healing, psychological change and growth. "If you can walk on fire, you can do anything you choose," I repeated after Tolly. I am in total agreement with him that "nothing limits us more than fear," and, although I understand that firewalking is not the only way to become free of fear, from my own experience I see that it is effective.

With recent widespread interest in firewalking, I have also been thinking of another intriguing possibility. It has long been known that Greek fire dancers *"consider themselves healers of all the community."* Similar beliefs and attitudes are widespread in other parts of the world where firewalking and fire dancing are practiced as a ritual. I am far from endorsing the claims of Transcendental Meditation (TM) advocates, that the practice of TM by many individuals creates an inexplicable effect of the "social field" which results in reduced accidents, illness, and crime (as measured by statistical social indicators) in their communities. But, since I have become better acquainted with firewalking, my thoughts keep returning to the possibility that firewalking has equal potential to play this role. After all, many ancient legends and rituals have already been found to be based on facts, rather than on people's imagination. Why not another one?

I believe that studying firewalking (both traditional and contemporary practices) will lead us to a better understanding of the mechanisms of psychic healing and self-healing, especially in the light of the above suggestions by J.C. Pearce, A. Weil and others that "firewalking involves the same process as innate healing." Now all my interests came together: along with conducting firewalking seminars, I started again teaching "energy" or "psychic" healing (some of my healing seminars end with a firewalk). I am also happy to see that many participants of firewalking seminars are extremely interested in exploring the spiritual implications of firewalking and regard the seminar as a profound spiritual experience. At the same time, most of the participants clearly understand that firewalking is by no means the ultimate goal, but just the beginning to self-exploration, personal transformation, and a better understanding of ourselves, our consciousness, and the universe.

Although my firewalking adventure has not solved all my problems of adjusting to a "new life," it has done much to put them into a different perspective. Sometimes I still feel a deep sadness, on the verge of tears—for I left behind my parents, my friends... and I left Barbara. However, I do know that now I am free to seek and explore further, and I value freedom. I believe in human potential, the potential of free individuals to find missing links within ourselves, between ourselves, and with the world beyond which we know very little about.

San Francisco
January, 1986

Larissa Vilenskaya performing a healing

"Transcending the limits"

■ VII.
Bibliography

Bibliography

I. Publications by Barbara Ivanova
(Selected Bibliography)

■ In this section we present a list of selected publications by Barbara Ivanova—in English as well as in other languages. Some titles are given in their original languages and some in English translation (in brackets) with indication of the language of the original.

1. Ivanova, B. "Guarizioni a distanza," *Metapsichica* (Rivista Italiana di Parapsicologia), Vol. XXIX, Fasc. I–II, January-June 1974, pp. 28–32 [in Italian].

2. Ivanova, B. [Investigations on Reincarnation—Methods of Its Application in the USSR]. *Ultra* (Finland), No. 1, 1974 [in Finnish].

3. Ivanova, B. "Reencarnation: su base fisiologica y biologica," *Conocimento de la nueva Era*, No. 441, Buenos Aires, September 1974 [in Spanish].

4. Ivanova, B. [Intuitive Forecasting: Experimental and Training Work], *Proceedings of the Second International Congress on Psychotronic Research,* Monte Carlo, 1975, pp. 322–325 [in Russian].

5. Ivanova, B. "Uutisia Neuvosto-liitosta," *Ultra*, No. 5, 1975 [in Finnish].

6. Ivanova, B. "Reincarnaation ja parantaminen," *Ultra*, No. 9, 1975 [in Finnish].

7. Ivanova, B. "L'azione bioenergetica quale energoir versione biologica," *Dimensione Psi* (Genova), Vol. I, July-December 1975, p. 15 [in Italian].

8. Ivanova, B. "Biologisch-kosmische Stralungshypcthesen," *Gnostisch-philosophische Parapsichologie* (Wien), Nos. 25, 26, 27, 19 6 [in German].

9. Ivanova, B. "Kuleshova and Kulagina," *International Journal of Paraphysics*, Vol. 11, No. 1/2, 1977, pp. 6–9.

10. Ivanova, B. "By-products of Psi," *International Journal of Paraphysics*, Vol. 11, No. 5/6, 1977, pp. 117–118.

11. Ivanova, B. "Experimental and Training Work on Some Group (Mass) Harmonizing Processes with Educating, Creativity-heightening and Healing Results," *Proceeding of the Third International Congress on Psychotronic Research,* Tokyo, 1977, pp. 463–471.

12. Ivanova, B. "Comment apprendre à se souvenir du futur: Methode

d'entrainement à la précognition." *Psi Réalités* (Paris), No. 10, 1978, pp. 24–27 [in French].

13. Ivanova, B. "Psycho- and Auto-Regulation," *International Journal of Paraphysics*, Vol. 12, No. 1/2, 1978, pp. 20–21.

14. Ivanova, B. "Krokhalev Interviewed," *International Journal of Paraphysics*, Vol. 12, No. 1/2, 1978, pp. 28–30.

15. Ivanova, B. "Psychography in the USSR," *International Journal of Paraphysics*, Vol. 12, No. 3/4, 1978, pp. 80–86.

16. Ivanova, B. "Cosmic Irradiations in (Mass) Healing Process: A Manifestation of Micro and Macro Cosmos Unity," *Proceedings of Fourth International Congress on Psychotronic Research*, São Paulo, Brazil, 1979, pp. 85–88.

17. Ivanova, B. "Cosmic Irradiations in (Mass) Healing Process: A Manifestation of Micro and Macro Cosmos Unity," in *Mind Over Matter*, by Walter & Mary Jo Uphoff, Oregon, Wis.: New Frontiers Center, 1980, pp. 245–247.

18. Ivanova, B. "Paranormale Heilung," *Allgemeine Zeitschrift für Parapsychologie* (Hamburg), No. 2, 1980 [in German].

19. Ivanova, B. "Some Soviet Views on 'Reincarnation'," *International Journal of Paraphysics*, Vol.14, No. 3/4, 1980, pp. 95–96.

20. Ivanova, B. "Relation of Paraphenomena to Physical Fields," *International Journal of Paraphysics*, Vol. 14, No. 5/6, 1980, pp. 110–112.

21. Ivanova, B. "Theoretical Concepts of Distant Healing and Clairvoyant Diagnostics," *Psychic Observer* (Washington, D.C.), Vol. 39, No. 3, 1981, pp. 225–231.

22. Ivanova, B. "Information-Bearing PK (Psychokinesis)," *New Frontiers Center Newsletter* (Oregon, Wis.), No. 1, January–March 1982, pp. 2–3.

23. Ivanova, B. "You Will Never See Your Son...," *Psi Research* (San Francisco, Ca.), Vol. 1, No. 2, June 1982, p. 102.

24. Ivanova, B. "Psychic Healing and Clairvoyant Diagnosis," *Light* (England), Vol. 102, No. 4, 1982.

25. Ivanova, B. "The Biolocation Effect and Distant Influence of the Biofield," *Psi Research*, Vol. 2, No. 3, September 1983, pp. 9–20.

26. Ivanova, B. "Some Experiments on Healing Processes," *Proceedings of the Fifth International Conference on Psychotronic Research*, Vol. 2, Bratislava, 1983, pp. 20–26.

27. Ivanova, B. "Some Training Experiments in Clairvoyance," *Proceedings of the Fifth International Conference on Psychotronic Research*, Vol. 3, Bratislava, 1983, pp. 162–167.

28. Ivanova, B., & Vilenskaya, L. "Aberdagem ao problema da reencarnação, considerada do ponto de vista biológico e fisico. Experiencias e hipóteses," *Reformador* (Brazil), July 1981 [in Portuguese].

29. Vilenskaya L., Ivanova V. [I Remember as it Was Some 1,000 Years Ago], *Volzhsky komsomolets* (city of Kuibyshev), October 11, 1975 [in Russian].

30. Vilenskaya, L., & Ivanova, B. [Is It Possible to Be Born Twice?] *Krug* (Israel), No. 132, 1979 [in Russian].

II. Publications on Research and Activities of Barbara Ivanova

(Selected Bibliography)

■ This section presents a selected bibliography of articles and books which (entirely or in part) describe Barbara Ivanova's work and situation. The books and articles, which were written by other researchers, reporters, or writers, are of differing degrees of accuracy. The fact that a particular book or article is included in the list does not mean that we confirm or endorse it.

1. Giovetti, P. "L'attivita della scienziata russa Barbara Ivanova," *Arcani* (Milan), Vol. VI, No. 6, June 1977, p. 62 [in Italian].
2. Giovetti, P. "Prodotti collaterali della psi," *Arcani* (Milan), Vol. VII, No. 12, December 1978, pp. 56–57 [in Italian].
3. Giovetti, P. "Barbara Ivanova, guaritrice chiaroveggente," *Arcani* (Milan), Vol. VIII, No. 6, June 1979, pp. 61–62 [in Italian].
4. Gris, H., & Dick, W. *The New Soviet Psychic Discoveries.* New York: Warner Books, 1979.
5. Locher, Theo. "Parapsicologia: problema politico in URSS," *Arcani* (Milan), Vol. X, No. 2, February 1981, pp. 36–39 [in Italian].
6. Passian, Rudolf. "Die Frau mit den heilenden Händen" [The Woman with Healing Hands], *Heim und Welt*, No. 15, April 4, 1974 [in German].
7. Passian, Rudolf. "Fernheilung: zwischen UdSSR und USA" [Distant Healing: Between the USSR and USA], *Esotera*, No. 6, 1974 [in German].
8. Passian, Rudolf. "Erziehung durch Erinnerungen an Frühere Leben. Neue Methoden und Anwedungsberiehe der Reinkarnationsforschung. Interview mit der russischen Parapsychologin Barbara Iwanova," *Esotera*, July 1974 [in German].
9. "Psi in Action," *Psi Research* (San Francisco, CA), Vol. 1, No. 1, March 1982, pp. 39–40.
10. Vilenskaya, Larissa. "Barbara Ivanova: Research Results and Present Difficulties," in *Parapsychology in the USSR*, Part I, L. Vilenskaya (Ed.), San Francisco: Washington Research Center, 1981, pp. 34–38.

III. Psi Research in the Soviet Union
(Selected Bibliography)

■ In this section we list a number of journals, articles, and books on Soviet psi research. The publications are of diverse scientific levels and of differing values. The fact that a particular book or article is included in the list does not mean that we confirm or endorse it.

A. Books

1. Dubrov, A.P., & Pushkin, V.N. *Parapsychology and Contemporary Science*, New York: Plenum, 1982.
2. Gris, H., & Dick, W. *The New Soviet Psychic Discoveries*, New York: Warner Books, 1979.
3. Ebon, M. *Psychic Warfare: Threat or Illusion*, New York: McGraw-Hill, 1983.
4. Krippner, S. *Human Possibilities: Mind Exploration in the USSR and Eastern Europe*, Garden City, N.Y.: Anchor, 1980.
5. Naumov, E., & Vilenskaya, L. *Bibliography of Parapsychology (Psychotronics, Psychoenergetics, and Psychobiophysics) and Related Problems, USSR*, Alexandria, Va.: Parapsychological Association, 1981.
6. Ostrander, S., & Schroeder, L. *Psychic Discoveries Behind the Iron Curtain*, Englewood Cliffs, N.J.: Prentice-Hall, 1970.
7. Ostrander, S., & Schroeder, L. *Handbook of PSI Discoveries*, New York: G.P. Putnam's Sons, 1974.
8. Ostrander, S., & Schroeder, L. *The ESP Papers: Scientists Speak Out from Behind the Iron Curtain*, New York: Bantam, 1976.
9. Vasiliev, L.L. *Experiments in Mental Influence*, New York: Dutton, 1976.
10. Vilenskaya, L. (Ed.) *Parapsychology in the USSR*, Parts I–V, San Francisco: Washington Research Center, 1981.

B. Journals

1. *International Journal of Paraphysics*, Benson Herbert (Ed.), Downton, Wiltshire, England.
2. *Psi Research* (An East-West Journal on Parapsychology, Psychotronics, and Psychobiophysics), Larissa Vilenskaya (Ed.), 3101 Washington St., San Francisco, Ca. 94115.

C. Articles

1. Adamenko, V. "Human Control of a Bioelectric Field," in S. Krippner & D. Rubin (Eds.) *The Energies of Consciousness*, New York: Gordon & Breach, 1975, pp. 75–78.

2. Adamenko, V. "Psi and Physical Fields," in W.G. Roll (Ed.), *Research in Parapsychology 1978*, Metuchen, N.J.: Scarecrow Press, 1979, pp. 75–77.

3. Bakirov, A. "On Certain Possible Uses of the Biophysical Method for Locating Useful Minerals," *International Journal of Paraphysics*, Vol. 12, No. 1/2, 1978, pp. 16–19.

4. Cassirer, M. "Experiments with Nina Kulagina," *Journal of the Society for Psychical Research*, Vol. 47, No. 759, March 1974, pp. 315–318.

5. Kitaev, N., & Ermakov, N. "Usage of Parapsychology in Criminal Investigation," *International Journal of Paraphysics*, Vol. 12, No. 5/6, 1978, pp. 111–116.

6. Krippner, S., & Davidson, R. "Parapsychology in the USSR," *Saturday Review*, March 18, 1972, pp. 56–60.

7. Krivorotov, V.K., Krivorotov, A.K., & Krivorotov, V.K. "Bioenergotherapy and Healing," *Psychoenergetic Systems*, Vol. 1, No. 1, 1974, pp. 27–30.

8. Moss T. "Psychic Research in the Soviet Union," in *Psychic Exploration: A Challenge for Science*, E.D. Mitchell & J. White (Eds.), New York: G.P. Putnam's Sons, 1974, pp. 469–486.

9. "Parapsychology in the Soviet Union," Special Issue, *International Journal of Parapsychology*, 1965.

10. Pratt, J.G., & Keil, H.H.J. "Firsthand Observations of Nina S. Kulagina Suggestive of PK Upon Static Objects," *Journal of the American Society for Psychical Research*, Vol. 67, 1973, pp. 381–390.

11. Ryzl, M. "Parapsychology in Communist Countries of Europe," *International Journal of Parapsychology*, Vol. 10, No. 3, 1968, pp. 263–276.

12. Vilenskaya, L. "Psi Research in the Soviet Union: Are They Ahead of Us?" in R. Targ, & K. Harary, *The Mind Race: Understanding and Using Psychic Abilities*, New York: Villard/Random House, 1984, pp. 247–260.

13. Wortz, E.C., Bauer, A.S., Blackwelder, R.F., Eerkens, J.W., & Saur, A.J. "An Investigation of Soviet Psychical Research," in *Mind at Large: Institute of Electrical and Electronic Engineers Symposia on the Nature of Extrasensory Perception*, C.T. Tart, H.E. Puthoff, & R. Targ (Eds.), New York: Praeger Press, 1979, pp. 235–260.

14. Zinchenko, V.P., Leontiyev, A.N., Lomov, B.F., & Luria, A.R. "Parapsychology: Fiction or Reality," in S. Krippner (Ed.), *Psychoenergetic Systems*, New York: Gordon & Breach, 1979.

15. Zlokazov, V., Pushkin, V., & Shevchuk, E. "Bioenergetic Aspects of the

Relationship Between the Image of Perception and the Perceived Object,"
Psi Research, Vol. 1, No. 3, September 1982, pp. 11–21.

IV. Suggestions for Further Reading

■ The following books can be of assitance to you (in addition to
the references to particular articles in this book) if you wish to
become acquainted with the fascinating world of psi phenomena in
more detail.

1. Bird, C. *The Divining Hand: The 500-year-old Mystery of Dowsing*, New
York: Dutton, 1979.
2. Eisenbud, J. *The World of Ted Serios*, New York: Morrow, 1967.
3. Krippner, S., & White, J. (Eds.) *Future Science: Life Energies and the Physics
of Paranormal Phenomena*, Garden City, N.Y.: Anchor, 1977.
4. Mishlove, J. *Roots of Consciousness*, New York: Random House, 1975.
5. Mitchell, E. & White, J. (Eds.) *Psychic Exploration: A Challenge for Science*,
New York: Putnam's, 1974.
6. Taylor, J. *Superminds*, Viking Press, 1975.
7. Targ, R., & Harary, K. *The Mind Race: Understanding and Using Psychic
Abilities*, New York: Villard/Random House, 1984.
8. Targ, R., Puthoff, H. *Mind-Reach: Scientists Look at Psychic Ability*, New
York: Delacorte Press, 1977.
9. Tomkins, P., & Bird, C. *The Secret Life of Plants*, New York: Harper &
Row, 1973.
10. Uphoff, W., & Uphoff, M. *Mind Over Matter*, Oregon, Wis.: New
Frontiers Center, 1980.

■ If you are interested in a more serious study of the field of psi
research, the following publications might be of assistance. Please
bear in mind that Saybrook Institute, Department of Consciousness
Studies (San Francisco, Ca.) and John F. Kennedy University (Or-
inda, Ca.) offer courses on parapsychology and consciousness
studies. A list of courses and study opportunities in parapsychology
can be obtained from the American Society for Psychical Research:
5 West 73rd Street, New York, NY 10023.

1. Jahn, R.G. (Ed.) *The Role of Consciousness in the Physical World*, Boulder,
Co.: Westview Press, 1981.

2. Krippner, S. (Ed.) *Advances in Parapsychological Research*, Vol. 1 (Psychokinesis). New York: Plenum, 1977.

3. Krippner, S. (Ed.) *Advances in Parapsychological Research*, Vol. 2, New York: Plenum, 1978.

4. Krippner, S. (Ed.) *Advances in Parapsychological Research*, Vol. 3, New York: Plenum, 1982.

5. Krippner, S. (Ed.) *Advances in Parapsychological Research*, Vol. 4, Jefferson, N.C.: McFarland, 1984.

6. Pucharich, A. (Ed.) *The Iceland Papers*, Amherst, Wis.: Essentia Research Associates, 1979.

7. Tart, C.T., Puthoff, H.E., & Targ, R. (Eds.) *Mind at Large: Institute of Electrical and Electronic Engineers Symposia on the Nature of Extrasensory Perception*, New York: Praeger Press, 1979.

8. Ryzl, M. *Parapsychology: A Scientific Approach.* New York: Hawthorn, 1970.

9. Ullman, M., & Krippner, S. *Dream Telepathy.* New York: Macmillan, 1975.

10. Wolman, B.B. (Ed.), *Handbook of Parapsychology*, New York: Van Nostrand Reinhold, 1977.

■ VIII.
Glossary

Glossary

Acupuncture An ancient Chinese system of medicine that uses needles inserted in the body at prescribed sites to stimulate the flow of chi (life energy) and thereby allegedly restores balance to the energy system that is thought to determine health. Modern variants of the original system use sound, lasers, chemicals, and massage on the acupuncture points.

Automatic Writing A motor automatism in which a person's hand writes meaningful statements, but without the writer consciously premeditating the content of what is produced.

Bioinformation Term used for extrasensory perception in the literature of Soviet and Eastern European parapsychology.

Biosphere "Sphere of life," a concept of global interconnectedness between all living beings on the Earth proposed by Soviet academician Vernadsky. It resembles the concept of "noosphere" developed by French philosopher Teilhard de Chardin.

Chakras Sanskrit for "wheel," receive their name from their appearance, which resembles vortices. In yogic philosophy, chakras are psychic centers in the body, generally dormant, which can be activated by kundalini, resulting in the attainment of psychic powers. Altogether there are ten chakras—visible only to clairvoyants—but of these it is advisable to use only seven. They are situated as follows: (1) the top of the head, (2) between the eyebrows, (3) the throat, (4) the heart, (5) the spleen, (6) the solar plexus, (7) the base of the spine. The remaining three chakras are situated in the lower part of the pelvis and normally are not used. Some traditions maintain that the chakras are nerve ganglia in the physical body; others maintain they reside in the astral (energy) body and are associated with various glands or organs in the physical body. A number of contemporary sensitives and psi researchers view chakras as centers of "energy exchange" between the body and environment, which (together with acupuncture points and meridians) form the body's energy system.

Clairaudience Paranormal information expressed as an auditory experience; it is generally considered to be a form or mode of clairvoyance.

Clairvoyance Paranormal acquisition of information concerning an object or contemporary physical event. In contrast to telepathy, the information is assumed to derive directly from an external physical source (such as a concealed photograph), and not from the mind of another person. As one particular form of extrasensory perception, it is not to be confused with the interpretation of clairvoyance as meaning "knowledge of the future" (see precognition). The term is sometimes used as "precognitive clairvoyance" or "clairvoyance in the future," meaning the paranormal acquisition of information concerning a physical target which will come into existence at some time in the future.

Dermo-optic Perception Term used to refer to the ability to discriminate color and brightness by means of touch. Also known as "skin vision" and "cutaneous perception." Some modifications of dermo-optic perception demonstrated by Rosa Kuleshova and other sensitives in the USSR, i.e., identification of images without touching them or through opaque media, apparently represent a borderline between dermo-optic and clairvoyant perception.

Dowsing A form of clairvoyance in which underground water, minerals, or hidden objects are located by means of a divining (dowsing) rod, pendulum, or other instruments. Some practitioners use just their bare hands, without a gadget, or their mental images (deviceless dowsing).

Extrasenser (from Extrasensory perception) Soviet term for a sensitive or psychic.

Extrasensory Perception (ESP) The acquisition of information about an external event, object or influence (mental or physical; past, present or future) otherwise than through any of the known sensory channels; term used to embrace such phenomena as telepathy, clairvoyance, and precognition.

Healing, Psychic Healing apparently brought about by such non-medical means as the "laying-on of hands" and inexplicable according to contemporary medical science. A form of psychic healing is absent healing which is usually defined as psychic healing brought about when the healer and the patient are outside the sensory range of each other.

Karma The word karma means "action," and the doctrine of karma (common to Brahmanism, Buddhism and Theosophy) generally teaches that everything done is done for eternity, that, in short, "thou shalt reap as thou didst sow." The doctrine of karma must be considered in the light of the teaching of reincarnation. Adherents of this teaching maintain that karma results from previous incarnations and determines the form of the forthcoming incarnation.

Kirlian Photography A type of high-voltage, high-frequency photography, developed in the Soviet Union by Semyon and Valentina Kirlian. While some researchers believe that Kirlian photographs indicate the existence of hitherto unknown radiations or energy fields around living systems, others maintain that these photographs result from a well known physical process. Namely, they represent a record on photographic film of the so-called "corona discharge" of an object caused by ionization of the field surrounding the object.

Kundalini According to yogic philosophy, a nonphysical energy in the human body, derived from prana, which is capable of activating psychic centers called chakras. Its activation in individuals through practice of various spiritual disciplines is said to result in enlightenment, creativity, and psychic powers.

Paranormal Term applied to any phenomenon which in one or more respects exceeds the limits of what is deemed physically possible on current scientific assumptions; often used as a synonym for "psychic," "parapsychological," or "attributable to psi."

Parapictography Automatic drawing and painting, similar to automatic writing.

Parapsychology Term coined by Max Dessoir and adopted by J.B. Rhine to refer to the scientific study of paranormal phenomena, i.e., psi. Parapsychology is the branch of science which deals with extrasensory perception and psychokinesis—that is, behavioral or personal exchanges with the environment that are extrasensorimotor (not depending on the senses and muscles).

Poltergeist From the German literally meaning "noisy ghost." Various paranormal manifestations involving the unexplained movement or breakage of objects, the lighting of fires and other similar phenomena. The phenomena often seem to depend upon the presence of a particular individual, called a "focus," frequently an adolescent or child.

Prana A form of energy postulated in ancient Hindu texts as the basic life force. Prana is thought to exist outside the types of energy (electricity, magnetism, gravity, and the nuclear forces) known to Western science.

Precognition A form of extrasensory perception in which the target is some future event that cannot be deduced from normally known data in the present.

Psi A term to designate collectively paranormal (psychic) events or faculties, including extrasensory perception and psychokinesis. The purpose of the term "psi" is to suggest that extrasensory perception and psychokinesis might be different aspects of a single process, rather than distinct and essentially different processes.

Psyche The Greek word for soul. In current English usage it can mean soul or mind.

Psychic As a noun, "psychic" refers to an individual who possesses psi ability of some kind and to a relatively high degree; as an adjective, it is often applied to paranormal events, abilities, research, etc., and thus means "concerning or involving psi," or "parapsychological."

Psychic Surgery A form of psychic healing well known for its practice in the Philippines, in which diseased tissues are said to be removed without the use of surgical instruments, and bleeding, infection, etc. are inhibited paranormally. The term is also used of surgery in which the surgeon operates while in a trance, as performed by J. Arigo and other Brazilian exponents of this practice, usually using unsterilized knives as scalpels.

Psychography See "Automatic Writing."

Psychokinesis (PK) The direct influence of mind on a physical system without the mediation of any known physical energy or instrumentation—that is, the extramotor aspect of psi. Sometimes also called telekinesis.

Psychotronics Czech term for parapsychology presently often used in the Soviet Union and Eastern European countries, which embraces certain phenomena (e.g., communication between tissue cultures through electromagnetic radiation) not generally accepted as parapsychological. At the same time, it usually does not include the study of phenomena pertaining to the concept of survival after death which are traditionally considered by parapsychology in the West.

Quasi-Auditory Perception A term coined by Barbara Ivanova for the phenomena of clairaudience. The term emphasizes that in this mode of perception an auditory experience is usually not of hallucinatory clarity, but often vague and indefinite.

Quasi-Visual Perception A term coined by Barbara Ivanova for the phenomena of clairvoyance. The term emphasizes that in this mode of perception a visual experience is usually not of hallucinatory clarity, but often vague and indefinite.

Reincarnation A concept suggesting that the human soul, or some aspects of self, is, after the death of the body, reborn into a new body, with this process being repeated throughout many lives.

Sensitive A person who is psychic—that is, is often able to induce psychic experience at will.

Telekinesis A form of psychokinesis, the movement of stationary objects without the use of any known physical force.

Telepathy Term coined by F.W.H. Myers to refer to the paranormal acquisition of information concerning the thoughts, feelings or activity of another conscious being; the word has superseded earlier expressions such as "thought-transference."

H. S. Dakin Company

3220 Sacramento Street • San Francisco, CA 94115

Publications (Partial List)

High Voltage Photography, by H. S. Dakin, 79 pp. 1975, $5.95.

Kundalini—Psychosis or Transcendence? by L. Sannella, M.D., 118 pp. 1976, $4.95.

Creativity in Education: The Waldorf Approach, by René Querido, 88 pp. 1984, 2nd printing, $5.95.

Publications of Earth Island Institute, Distributed by HSDC (Partial List)

The First Biennial Conference On the Fate of the Earth: Conservation and Security In a Sustainable Society, New York, 1982, 497 pp. Published 1983, $12.00.

The Second Biennial Conference On the Fate of the Earth, Peace On and With the Earth For All Its Children, Washington, D.C., 1984, 628 pp. Published 1985, $12.00.